Things
That
Work

Things That Work

A No-Nonsense Guide to Recovery by One Who Knows

Barry Bocchieri

Learning Publications, Inc.
Holmes Beach, Florida

ISBN 1-55691-176-9

Learning Publications, Inc.
5351 Gulf Drive
P.O. Box 1338
Holmes Beach, FL 34218-1338

Printing: 5 4 3 2 1   Year: 4 3 2 1 0

Printed in the United States of America

Dedication

This book is dedicated to all the friends of Bill W., past and present, alive and dead, without whose help this book never would have been written. To all my brothers and sisters in the Program, this book is also for you. To Bill K., sorry you couldn't make the trip, buddy, but my spirit is with you. To my sponsor, Carl G., who is now with Higher Power, I also dedicate this book to you, because if it weren't for you, I would have been dead. And to every poor soul who suffers, did suffer, or will ever suffer from this dreadful disease, I dedicate this book. It is for all of you, for us.

To Mom, who is now with Higher Power, and Dad. I knew it would come; it just took a little longer, that's all. Thanks for believing in me.

Dedication

Contents

Acknowledgments

A book, like any creative enterprise, is a collective endeavor. Many people contributed to the completion of this project.

First off, I would like to thank my current copy editor and editorial consultant, Shirley Foor, for her guidance and attention to detail. Much thanks. To my current typist, Patty Shannon, deep gratitude for the final draft.

To my early typists, Sally Herrmann and Karen Brenney, deep gratitude for transferring what I wrote to the printed word.

To my friends who have read the manuscript and given me what I needed most — feedback — I would like to thank Sandy, Michael, and Don.

For professional guidance I would like to thank Martin Galatine and Don Grigg.

To my early copy editor, Katherine Balch, much help in shaping the early manuscript to form.

And to all the other people who have contributed in one way or another, who are too numerous to mention, thanks. You know who you are. I wouldn't have been able to do it without you.

Introduction

This book is for the alcoholic who is beginning to come to terms with his problem. It contains no generalities behind which you can hide, no Pollyanna solutions that will let you believe that you can sidestep the tough times ahead. Instead, you will have the principles that worked for me in spite of any predisposition for, inclination toward, and background of alcoholism I might have had.

Perhaps your counselor loaned you this copy to read in preparation for your next session. Perhaps a loved one gave it to you in fervent hope that something between these covers would reach into you and set you on the road to sobriety. Or, perhaps, you have decided to be the best friend you could be to yourself and learn to better understand the demons and the terrors of alcoholism, the excuses you make to yourself and others in your life, and the motivations for your drinking. Whatever your motivation for reading this, be very sure in your mind of two things: One, no matter how loudly and vigorously you protest, you are no different from any other alcoholic. You have gone through or will go through the same stages of denial and anger and relapse that every other alcoholic has experienced. Two, the arduous trip from alcoholism to sobriety will tempt you to believe that you are different and to take some misleading and unproductive side journeys. I know this from experience.

In my search, I found many ideas that worked and many that did not. I was helped by some and hurt by others. Hopefully, my experiences as an alcoholic who has been sober for more than 18 years and as a counselor of alcoholics will be detailed clearly enough to help you. Within this small book are some of the ideas and the methods that helped me to experience and to deal with sobriety. Learning to live with sobriety — the quality of being sober — takes a firm decision, serious determination, continual practice, and perseverance, because we alcoholics take great care to avoid that state, often for years. I began drinking when I was in junior college to feel grown up and to be part of the crowd. I liked the feeling that alcohol gave me. When I drank, I didn't have to worry. I felt free. Free is the operative word. You might have started drinking to be free from abuse, or free from emotional or physical pain, or free from the terrible "wrongs" that life has visited upon you. What is true is, that when we, you and I, slipped into alcoholism, we gave over this "freedom" from whatever we feared or gave us pain to the slavery of alcohol. Regardless of what "reason" for drinking that we used, we, you and I, consciously decided to drink. No one forced us to drink.

During my twenties, my tolerance for alcohol grew and so did my drinking. By age 29, I thought my life was over. In addition to drinking alcohol, I had begun to smoke pot and to experiment with drugs. Little did I know that I was headed for trouble with alcohol. We alcoholics are the last to know about our trouble with alcohol because we keep it such a secret from ourselves. Preserving the secret is the only way we can continue our drinking. As my drinking increased, so did my drug consumption. I was on prescription drugs, but I complicated the efforts of my physician by continuing to drink alcohol and smoke pot. I was in trouble. I suffered from panic attacks, and I could not hold a job.

When I entered the first treatment facility, my life was, as we say in 12-step treatment, completely unmanageable. I had attempted suicide and was admitted to psychiatric hospitals and to alcohol and drug rehabilitation centers, only to undergo years of therapy from psychiatrists, counselors, and psychologists — none of whom were very effective in changing my habits.

Today, however, I have been sober and "clean" for the past 18 years. No booze. No pot. No illicit drugs of any kind. It took me two years to get sober and still more time to break the addiction to the prescription drugs and the pot and more time still to rebuild a life without these addictions. For the past seven years, I have had a successful practice in counseling alcoholics and training other counselors and alcoholism professionals in the disease of alcoholism and the nature of recovery.

What happened to change my habits? These are the things that I shall share with you. The good with the bad. The bitter with the sweet. I know what it is like to be in the worst stages of alcoholism, as well as in the recovery stage. The principles I present in these chapters can help you to get sober, to live without alcohol and drugs, to live with and deal with the long-term problems associated with sobriety, and to make the most of your life without alcohol or other mind-altering drugs. We shall work through what sobriety is and not impose the myths and the ideas of what sobriety is supposed to be. We can end the disease if we can face what life is without the disease.

The 12-step programs are described, along with therapies that have worked for me and for many other alcoholics. Without a doubt, sobering up and maintaining sobriety bear their complications, but I promise you something from deep down in my heart: If you embrace the ideas in this book and practice the methods, you will see results. Keep in mind, however, that the results will be in direct proportion to your effort.

The first chapter begins with the importance of accepting alcoholism as a disease and the stages of alcoholism. The succeeding chapters will detail the events and the changes that occur from the first attempts at sobering up to achieving sobriety. Hopefully, some of what you read will help you to understand more clearly and to begin your journey toward sobriety.

1
An Understanding
of Alcoholism

Before we move on to thinking about alcoholism as a disease, we need to understand alcoholism itself. Of all the definitions of alcoholism, the one I favor appears in the *Big Book of Alcoholics Anonymous:* "If, when you honestly want to, you find you cannot quit entirely, or if, when drinking you have little control over the amount you take, you are probably an alcoholic." This definition is pertinent because, once an alcoholic starts drinking, he cannot predict his behavior with any degree of certainty. No one in the family or his circle of friends can predict an alcoholic's behavior with any certainty, either. Sometimes, an alcoholic can be as nonaggressive as the proverbial church mouse and nothing serious occurs. Sometimes, the alcoholic becomes aggressive or reckless. Sometimes, the alcoholic just cries or turns into a raging animal. There is, of course, the alcoholic who might say, "Where do I fit in? I drink at home, and I don't bother anybody." Because the patterns of drinking and of behavior are unpredictable among alcoholics, understanding these variations is not easy, except when we look at them in terms of the conditions that accompany alcoholism: physical compulsion, mental obsession, and progression of alcoholic tendencies.

Alcoholism As a Disease

We can understand alcoholism as a disease a little better if we look at the nature of disease and the two forces that drive the alcoholic: obsession and compulsion.

One dictionary definition describes disease "as a condition of an organ, part, structure, or system of the body in which there is incorrect function resulting from the effect of heredity, infection, diet, or environment." You do not, for instance, have to "catch" an illness in order for you to have a disease. You don't "catch" Alzheimer's, but you would have a disease. Cancer appears randomly in the body. Scientists are unsure how or why that happens, but it is pretty safe to say that it is not a communicable disease, such as tuberculosis, hepatitis, or measles. The predisposition to alcoholism could be hereditary, or it could result from a combination of factors, none of which you "caught" from someone else.

Regardless of how the alcoholic comes to have the disease, he faces the tyranny of obsession and compulsion. Obsession is a malady of the mind, whereas compulsion is a disorder of the body. The compulsion is, however, a factor that prevents many therapists and lay persons from understanding that alcoholism is a disease. The idea of compulsion leads them to believe that alcoholism results solely from physiological needs.

The compulsion begins when alcohol triggers a biochemical process that pressures you, the alcoholic, to drink, despite the fact that, on a cognitive level, you might not want to drink. Once the biochemical process is triggered, taking that first drink is the only thing that you can think about. Still, "one drink is too many and 1,000 isn't enough," as recovering alcoholics tell each other. Moreover, will power, which your well-meaning friends will suggest that you use, will be ineffective. As Father Martin, a leader in the field of alcoholism says, "The next time you think will power works, try to use it on diarrhea." (Martin 1989) The need for an alcoholic to avoid the disastrous affects of the first drink has made Alcoholics Anonymous (AA) and the therapists who use a 12-step program in their treatment as effective as they are. "It is the first drink that gets you drunk," says one AA slogan. "If you don't pick up the first drink, you can't get drunk." The physical compulsion is the easiest to treat. Give up drinking, or enter a hospital or detoxification unit for two to five days, or until the compulsion wears off.

The obsession is distinctly different from the physically driven compulsion. With the obsession, the desire to drink takes over the alcoholic's thoughts and feelings. Thoughts about taking the alcohol, feeling the effect of the first drink, feeling free, even the act of holding the glass, consume your every thought. You cannot walk away from an obsession, as you can the physical compulsion. Each alcoholic is subject to the craving for a drink. AA meetings promote a good technique to use to reduce the effect of obsession. The technique is honesty, or owning up to "character defects." Alcoholism is a character defect. When you own that defect, when you honestly own your alcoholism, emotionally and mentally, and say the words, the obsession loses some of its power.

As with other diseases, alcoholism has observable beginning, middle, and end stages. Alcoholism is a problem unto itself. Furthermore, as with cancer or heart disease, alcohol can become a terminal illness without proper intervention. Untreated, the alcoholic's physical, mental, and social condition will worsen until the condition exceeds any treatment. It is easier to understand the idea that alcoholism can become a terminal illness if we examine the stages that alcoholics go through without effective intervention.

Stage 1 (The Adaptive Stage)

The Adaptive Stage, the beginning stage, is characterized by two basic components (Jellinek 1960). As you adapt to your alcoholism, your tolerance for alcohol is increased. For instance, if you got drunk on one six pack of beer, and your drinking goes unchecked, then, say, three years later, you might need three six packs to reach the same state of drunkenness. Your tolerance for alcohol has increased. The second characteristic of the Adaptive Stage is that you have begun to exhibit slight withdrawal symptoms, such as depression, anxiety, and agitation. Such symptoms result after you have temporarily stopped drinking, usually the morning after, but they might even persist throughout the day. Sometimes, these symptoms are confused with psychological or personality problems, but they are related entirely to your withdrawal from the alcohol.

Stage 2 (The Dependent Stage)

In the middle stag, the Dependent Stage, two levels of events tend to occur: blackouts and loss of control. (Perhaps you will recognize some familiar experiences, but we hope you have not reached this point in your disease.) A blackout is amnesia that is brought on by the abusive consumption of alcohol. You don't just lose consciousness; you experience a loss of memory as a result of your drinking. Blackouts can be as short as moments or as long as several days. Stories about alcoholics being unable to remember driving home from a bar are legion. An alcoholic can lose complete days, an entire sequence of events. For example, a friend was driving home after he had been drinking all night. He experienced a blackout, just as he realized that he was going to make a wrong turn. The next thing he realized was that he was making the wrong turn again; he blacked out again. It was nightmarish. He relived the scene over and over again until he got it right. How my friend got home, or how he got on the right road, I do not know; neither does he. He did, however, make it home safely. My friend had been sober 20 years when he told me that story. There are stories about people building houses, flying planes, teaching classes, all in a blackout condition.

The loss of control over your drinking is another symptom of the Dependent Stage. If, for example, you tell your family or friends that you are going to have one beer, and you end up drinking 20 beers, you have experienced a severe loss of control. Bill Wilson, a cofounder of AA, tells this story on himself that emphasizes the loss of control. He had been sober for a short period of time, and, while he was sober, he was exposed to a medical theory about allergies, mental obsession, and physical compulsion before he took a bus trip. The bus stopped for lunch at a restaurant that served alcoholic beverages. The person who had been sitting next to him on the bus ordered a scotch and soda; Bill ordered a ginger ale. After Bill told his companion about alcohol creating a physical allergy, he looked at his friend's scotch, back at his ginger ale, and said, "I'll have a scotch." The man said, "You are going to have a drink after everything you told me?" Bill said, "Yes." The man said, "You're sick!" At which point Bill looked at his companion and said, "I know." With that, Bill went on a three-week binge, during which he drew not a single sober breath. That's loss of control. Bill Wilson eventually sobered up and became a cofounder of AA.

During the Dependent Stage, withdrawal symptoms also begin to intensify. Hangovers increase, and severe anxiety and depression enter the picture. This is when many alcoholics develop phobias, as well as anxiety attacks or nameless fears. Often, the episodes occur in the morning, hovering over the alcoholic's bed like a mist. Paranoia increases, and the alcoholic begins to experience unreasonable resentments. Other symptoms might present themselves, but blackout and loss of control are the most common.

Stage 3 (The Deteriorative Stage)

The Deteriorative Stage is the last stage of alcoholism. This is the stage in which the alcoholic begins to experience life-threatening physical damage as a result of too much drinking. Because alcohol is a quicker source of fuel than is food, alcohol is processed first. The body tries to process alcohol like it processes food, but alcohol is not food. Any food already in the liver is digested after the body tries to digest the alcohol. Because the alcoholic is abusing the intake of alcohol, the body is unable to process much of the fat in the food. As a result, the fat is stored in the liver, and the liver's ability to filter toxins, the job for which the liver was designed, is seriously impaired. The deterioration has begun.

As the liver is unable to filter toxins, the level of liver enzymes increases and hepatitis develops. This type of hepatitis is thought to be noncontagious, but it definitely is common among alcoholics. Cirrhosis, a disease of the liver, is the next stage of deterioration. A liver in this condition loses still more of its ability to filter toxins and becomes leathery and scarred. If you have been diagnosed with cirrhosis of the liver and/or demonstrate the clinical symptoms mentioned above, alcoholism and alcoholic are words that should come to mind.

Deterioration comes in other forms, too. You might experience alcoholic polyneuropathy, which, in its early stages, produces a tingling sensation in the fingers and hands. This occurs because alcohol destroys the myelin sheath, which protects the nerves. If you continue to drink after these symptoms exhibit themselves, permanent destruction can result. In the early and middle stages, this condition can be treated with abstinence, proper diet, and the supplementation of certain vitamins, all under the guidance and oversight of the health-care professional, of course.

Other symptoms of deterioration that develop in Stage 3 are delirium tremens (DTs) and seizures or esophageal hemorrhages. During the DTs, the alcoholic sees and hears extraordinary things, such as pink elephants and little green men, or, more likely, horrible things, such as snakes and dragons. Alcoholics who suffer from the DTs, become feverish and sweaty. Although this condition might be frightening, seizures and esophageal hemorrhages (a hemorrhage in the esophagus that causes bleeding from mouth) can be fatal. If the alcoholic and his disease are left untreated, death may be imminent.

Differences Between Progression and Tolerance

Unlike tolerance, which is the ability to consume ever greater quantities of alcohol, progression among alcoholics describes the ability of the alcoholic to consume the same amount or more after a period of sobriety. For example, if you started drinking at 18 years of age, stopped at 28, was sober for 10 years and then started drinking again at age 38, you would be able to consume as much alcohol or more than if you had continued drinking during those 10 years.

Is Social Drinking Ever a Possibility?

Therapists disagree over whether an alcoholic can ever resume social drinking without dire consequences. However, people in AA, as well as a vast array of professionals in the field of alcoholism and addiction, are adamant. They contend that once an alcoholic, always an alcoholic. Or, as we say in treatment, "Once you're a pickle, you're never a cucumber again." The *Big Book of Alcoholics Anonymous* asserts that alcoholics are people who seem to have crossed an invisible line, and, once they have crossed it, they cannot return to social drinking without serious consequences.

Much of the controversy over whether an alcoholic can return to social drinking without losing control seems to center on Stage 1 alcoholics, or those in the Adaptive Stage. Bill Wilson addressed this point when he said, in describing Stage 1 alcoholics, "people are now entering the fellowship who are scarcely alcoholics." If you have any of the symptoms mentioned in these pages, you should see a trained alcoholism-treatment professional who can make a valid evaluation. Specifically, you should see a certified alcoholism counselor. You also should attend several AA meetings to see if you hear your story told through the words of someone in the group. Chances are that you will.

The Relevance of the Disease

Perhaps the most important point in this chapter is that the alcoholic is a sick person who, mostly, is trying to get well. The alcoholic is not a bad person who is trying to be a good person. The best way to become well is to identify the problem. The problem is alcoholism. Will power does not work, but abstaining from alcohol one day at a time does. Identifying the problem and facing the problem one day at a time are the cornerstones of the AA program and of most alcohol-treatment therapists. Keep the idea that alcoholism is a disease clearly in your mind. It will help to alleviate feelings of guilt. What you have done to your family, friends, employer, or to yourself should not matter at this point. What is important is to understand what your alcoholism is doing to you. If you grasp the idea that the alcoholic — you — is powerless, which will be discussed more fully in a later chapter, you will understand that you have little or no control without certain supports. You are powerless to stop your drinking without appropriate intervention.

Alcoholism Is Not a Moral Issue

Morality has little to do with alcoholism. Morality comes into play only when the alcoholic understands that he is an alcoholic and that something must be done about his alcoholism. It is then that the alcoholic is obligated to take action, to do something about his alcoholism. Even then, we believe that the key word is responsibility, not morality. Do not confuse responsibility with blame. Blame refers to someone calling attention to past actions, the actions of the alcoholic or of another person who "contributed" to the alcoholism, that were inappropriate; responsibility refers to taking constructive action to affect the present and the future. It is important to know the distinction between the two, so that you do not become confused and spend time blaming yourself or others. In this light, it takes great responsibility to accept alcoholism as a disease. If one is ill, one must take responsibility for improving one's health, or, in this case, accepting alcoholism as a disease and taking responsibility for becoming sober.

If you have any question about what stage of alcoholism you are in, please reread this chapter. We understand that if you are dependent upon alcohol for any reason, you have a disease. Only you can get rid of the disease, but you must accept responsibility for achieving your good health and accept the help of those who are experienced in and knowledgeable about "what works."

2
Denial Can Be Deadly

We alcoholics are very manipulative people. When it comes to making sure that we can continue our drinking, we are con artists extraordinaire. We can tell ourselves and everyone around us the most believable stories about how we are not alcoholics. We can even remember blacking out and losing control, and, yet, we'll call ourselves "social drinkers," not alcoholics. Some of us will tell ourselves that we aren't alcoholics because we always do our drinking at home and don't bother anyone. Black is white and up is down. Just ask us. We can make it so to keep drinking.

Aristotle, in clarifying the Law of Identity, overlooked us. The Law of Identity says, basically, that a thing is a thing, and it is not something else. A chair is a chair; it is not a bird or a bear. A rock is a rock; it is not a cloud or a clock. The alcoholic, however, is always something else. A "social drinker." A person with emotional problems. A person grieving for the loss of something. We always seem to persuade ourselves that we are not what we are. Our foundation for this phenomenon is solidly rooted in a single word of far-reaching proportions — denial. All of us, even the non-alcoholics, engage in denial from time to time. The difference between them and us is, we depend upon and cling to denial to continue our regular and abusive consumption of alcohol. Denial is key to our addiction.

Denial is a mechanism that manifests itself when things in our day-to-day life are too painful for us to face without alcohol. Much of our denial is unconscious. We have engaged in denial so long that it is as common as breathing. In her book *On Death and Dying,* Elizabeth Kubler Ross writes about the experiences terminally ill patients go through before they can accept the harsh reality of their fate. They face denial, bargaining, anger, and depression before they finally accept what is happening to them. Notice that the first phase is denial. Their fate is too painful, the loss too great, for them to accept, so they deny that it is happening. The person does not necessarily go through these phases in order. They might go from denial to acceptance to anger to bargaining to acceptance and back to denial. Nevertheless, they must negotiate all of the stages before they can fully accept. What does this stuff about death and dying have to do with you? Well, we alcoholics go through the same stages as we accept our alcoholism. In fact, in alcoholism treatment, we call this grieving for the loss of an old friend — the loss of our contact with our old friend alcohol.

Reality Will Persist

Although we can lie to ourselves and deny what we are doing, reality has a way of intruding, whether we like it or want it around. Reality is persistent in its attack on our subconscious, the home of much of our denial. If denial is largely unconscious, then what help is there for us? We can remember that nothing we do remains solely within or around us, and that today's denial will eventually topple our house of cards. Here's an example that I give in my seminars. A law in ecology says that everything is connected to everything else. What we do today in this place will affect someone else in another place. For instance, if a company burns fossil fuel in Youngstown, Ohio, and pollutes the atmosphere, the acid rain that comes down in the Adirondack Mountains, hundreds of miles away, pollutes the lakes and kills the fish. The burning of fluorocarbons in North America depletes the ozone layer at the North Pole. Harvesting the lumber in the tropical rain forests in the Amazon region affects the insects and the animals that live there. The same links exist with things of the mind. It is all connected. If I lie in one area of my life, the lie eventually will affect another area, even if that area seems unconnected to the original issue. What this means is, if I lie to my family about one topic, then it is easier for me to lie to myself about my drinking. I can kid myself — lie to myself — that it is OK for me to drink.

We know of only one antidote for denial. It is called honesty. We probably should write the word with an uppercase H, because Honesty is the cornerstone of our recovery from this disease called alcoholism. To hark back to the Law of Identity, we are alcoholics. We are not social drinkers, nor do we have emotional problems that bring on the drinking. We also are not bad people trying to be good people. We have a disease called alcoholism, and we are trying to get well. That is the Honesty of your life and of mine. Taking responsibility for the recovery from this disease is not much different from being lost in a dense woodland. We have a choice. We can deny that we are lost and let our denial send us deeper into the trees and underbrush, where we might very well perish, or we can accept the Honesty of the situation and make decisions that will lead us back to familiar ground. The same is true about dealing with our disease. We can deny that we have the disease and literally perish from the results of our denial, or we can take responsibility for our health.

Where Do We Begin?

We must be honest about two things: We are powerless over alcohol, and our lives are unmanageable when we drink alcohol. To be honest about our powerlessness is to acknowledge and to accept that we are addicted to alcohol and that, for us "One drink is too much and a thousand isn't enough." I once believed that I was different from all the other drinkers, but the honesty of my life is, I am not. For me, the honesty means that once I pick up the first drink, I will not be able to stop drinking. I am powerless over alcohol. As a result of my powerlessness, my life becomes unmanageable.

At age 29, my life was so unmanageable that I was admitted to my first rehabilitation center — the first of several. I had suffered for years from panic attacks, depression, explosive anger, low self-esteem, alienation, self-hate, and a catalog of other emotional and psychological problems. I was unemployable, having either quit or been fired from numerous jobs. I had persuaded myself that I drank because I had emotional problems. I believed that I drank because my life was unmanageable. In truth, my life was unmanageable because I drank to excess, because I was addicted to the alcohol. Honesty helped me to understand that when I surrender to the alcohol, I lose my freedom to make good decisions, to have lasting relationships, to have job security, and, in a phrase, to remain in control of my life. When I surrender to alcohol, I surrender to my disease. I had a choice, just as you do now. Instead of continuing to surrender to the alcohol, I surrendered to the truth of my life and of the disease. By recognizing that I am powerless over my addiction, I surrendered to win, to beat the disease. In the martial art Aikido, one learns to flow with the force of one's opponent in order that one might use the opponent's force against him. Once I understood the forces of my opponent (the disease of addiction to alcohol), I could use the force to defeat it. If I continued to deny that the opponent exists, I could do nothing to help myself.

Take the First Step Now

The same is true for you. In order to gain something that is valuable (your good health and control over your life), you must give up that which is problematic, even deadly. Once you accept the idea that you might be an alcoholic — an alcohol addict — then the first step toward your good health is to admit that you are powerless over your addiction and that your addiction has made your life unmanageable.

When you have accepted that you have a disease that makes your life unmanageable, bring your knowledge into the light. Tell someone you trust that you understand you have a disease, that you want to be well again, and that you are willing to take responsibility for your treatment. If you can't say the words out loud, give them life on paper. Write them and let this person you trust read them. The person might even be able to help you to say the words. When you bring your new awareness into the open, when you lay denial to rest, you may experience a sense of relief that is overwhelming. You might even cry. Let the tears come.

Taking the first step probably will open the door to some pain that you have been shutting away for years. Let the pain come, too. Acknowledging it, allowing it are part of the healing. I have learned through my experience with AA and with my clients that you will experience "a new freedom and a new happiness." This freedom and happiness reinforce the significance of taking the first step.

Take the Step One Day at a Time

There is only one thing that you must remember about taking the first step. You must take it every day, one day at a time. You must acknowledge every day that you are powerless over alcohol and that your life is unmanageable when you drink alcohol. You must avoid the first drink of alcohol every day because the first drink will not be your last. You cannot deny that you are an alcoholic.

If you have the gut-level desire to stop drinking, then trade denial for honesty about your addiction. If you have the gut-level desire to be in control of your life, then acknowledge and accept your powerlessness over alcohol. When you honestly acknowledge the truth of your life, you can begin to recover from your disease.

3
Honesty is Powerful

Before I stopped drinking, I went to many therapists. In fact, I went to so many therapists, marriage counselors, psychiatrists, and psychologists that the decade of my twenties was encapsulated in therapy. In all of those hours in all of those offices, not one of those professionals told me to be honest with myself. One did give me a choice, an ultimatum, actually. "Quit drinking or quit therapy." Being a good alcoholic, I quit therapy. I couldn't be honest with myself about my drinking, so I walked away from the therapist's ever-present reminders that I "might be" an alcoholic. When I entered alcohol treatment, the first thing I was told was to "get honest" with myself and to stop kidding myself. It was the first time those words had been put to me straight out. It took me some time, however, to grasp this powerful point.

Lying in order to continue drinking is so deep-seated in our minds that we alcoholics often don't even realize that we are lying. When we do know that we are lying, we aren't always so clever as we might think that we are about those lies. We even lie to ourselves about that. Shortly after I joined an alcoholism-treatment program, my sponsor

wanted me to attend a 12-step meeting with him. I went —
to a bar. I called my sponsor and told him that I couldn't go
to the meeting. I was so involved in my lie that I didn't realize my sponsor could hear the "bar noises," the ching-
ching of the shuffleboard machine, the tell-tale level of
conversation and raucousness, in the background. This was
the first time that someone had caught me squarely in my
lie and called me on it. Honesty began to have some reality
for me in the months to come.

How honest can you be? What do you remember
about times when you lied, and the other person probably
knew it? What about the lies to your family? To your employer? To your friends? You've been guilty of lying, even
if you are kidding yourself right now. Can you face the
truth about your addiction long enough to continue reading?

Honesty works to get beyond alcoholism for many
reasons. One of those reasons has to do with ethics, which
is the discipline of right and wrong. In my years in traditional therapy programs, I was told to focus on what I
wanted, not what was right. I wanted to take drugs. How
"right" with life was that course of action? When I entered
the 12-step program, my sponsor told me what was wrong
with doing what I wanted. Such willful and self-absorbed
behavior devalued me as a human being; I owed myself
more respect than I was giving. From my perspective, one
of the reasons that AA and other 12-step programs are successful is that they are value laden. The leaders don't tell
participants to do what they want, so long as they don't hurt
themselves or someone else. They say, instead, that you
must be emotionally honest with yourself in your decisions
and consider whether those decisions will endanger your

continued sobriety. Honesty may be the most important of the values, but the programs also emphasize willingness, open-mindedness, kindness, optimism and faith, among other values, which combine to make the alcoholic who desires to be free of his illness healthy again.

We alcoholics lie to ourselves to continue our drinking; we must, therefore, be honest with ourselves if we are to stop drinking. In a poem, W.E. Henley writes, "It matters not how straight the gate, How charged with punishments the scroll, I am the master of my fate; The captain of my soul." The ability to be honest about your addiction on a daily basis puts you in charge of your life. When you are honest, there is no room for denial.

Are Your Lips Moving?

In treatment, we ask, "How do you know if an addict is lying?" The answer is, "If his lips are moving." While this might sound cruel, the thought bears some truth. I have counseled the rich, and the mighty, and the poor, and the homeless. What they have in common, regardless of their socioeconomic differences, is their inability to be honest with themselves about their addiction. My advice to them is the same as my advice to you: Look inside yourself. Look into your conscience. Listen to that still, small voice that philosophers talk about. It has always been there, waiting for you to listen and to hear.

The idea that your conscience has a voice is not "psycho babble," the latest concept in whatever treatment devised to get you "to change your ways." You have, I am sure, heard the voice many times. "You should be home with your family, rather than sitting in this bar." "You are going to be too hung over in the morning to attend the

meeting if you keep drinking." "If you drink any more, you
have no business driving home." I probably should leave
space here for you to insert one or two of the many, many
messages your still, small voice has conveyed while you
tilted the glass toward your lips, or gripped the bottle to
pour yet another shot. Don't fall back into denial and say
that you never heard that voice. I heard it and made excuses. You have heard it and made excuses. That still, small
voice has the power to help you overcome your illness and
how to regain control over your life.

Introspection is Good for the Soul

The technique of listening to that inaudible voice is
called introspection, or "looking for the truth," as the mys-
tics describe it. Introspection has been practiced by every
great spiritual teacher from Jesus to Gandhi. During the
British occupation of India, Gandhi called for the people to
march to the sea in protest of the British tax on salt. During
the march, Gandhi changed his mind and called off the
march. Gandhi's supporters objected to his decision, saying
that he had an obligation to the people. Gandhi replied that
he had a dedication to the truth, as he understood it, on a
day-to-day basis, and that his understanding took prece-
dence over his obligation to the people. Gandhi was honest
with himself, and he listened to the inner clues about the
circumstances and events and did not let the pressures of
everyday living get in the way of his search for the truth.

Psychologists call this being inner directed. We look
inside for our sense of self-worth. To be outer directed is to
look outside of ourselves and be what is commonly called
"people pleasing." We look to other people to be our
source of strength, rather than finding it within ourselves.

Each of us possesses qualities that we both like and dislike. Still, honestly owning all of those qualities and responding to the best and most positive of them by listening to your conscience will help you to take the first step and to take that step each and every day thereafter.

This chapter might be brief, but we don't need a lot of words to say that honesty is powerful and that exchanging denial for honesty is the only way back to good health from your addiction.

4
The Basics

Before we begin some new interest in our lives, we must first learn the basics of the activity. For instance, we must learn the order of operations in general mathematics before we can tackle algebra. We must grasp the basics of operating a camera before we can produce photographs that are worth showing our friends. Before we can make sense of the words in our heads, we must know how to string those words together in some logical order so that our words can be understood. So it is, too, with freeing yourself from your addiction and gaining a healthy life.

A "basic" is an action or a belief, a simple foundation of thought, that enables you to do something else. We have talked about the importance of some of the fundamentals, such as knowing and understanding that alcoholism is a disease, recognizing your addiction, getting honest with yourself about that addiction, and taking the first concrete step toward sobriety — admitting that you are powerless over the alcohol and that your alcoholism has made your life unmanageable. Accepting and engaging these basics enables you to work on the other basics that are necessary to keep you on the road to sobriety.

Basic — Avoid Certain People, Places, and Things

The first fundamental is to avoid people, places, and things that are a threat to your sobriety. The operative words here are avoid and threat. Remember when your mother used to tell you "out of sight, out of mind"? Your mother offered you a valuable way to help you deal with some difficult times. Among alcoholics, certain persons, places or things, can trigger a relapse. These "relapse triggers" create the craving for alcohol. A craving is similar to the compulsion or the obsession that we talked about in an earlier chapter, and the craving is not confined to alcoholism. If you went to a bar, for instance, and drank a cola, chances are, you would eventually crave a drink. A gambler who goes to the racetrack just to "watch the horses run" probably will end up craving the thrill of the bet and race off to the betting window. Calling an old girlfriend or boyfriend just to say "hello" might sound innocent enough, but the sounds and the memories soon would trigger a craving for that person, that relationship, no matter how detrimental the action might be to your resolve to stay healthy. When you avoid the people, places, and things that threaten your good health and your sobriety, your life become easier, and a possible relapse remains farther away.

This concept is similar to the reality of denial. If you are honest with yourself, you know and admit that the particular person, place, or thing has a magnetism that will draw you from your sobriety into the bottle. If you avoid these relapse triggers, you will avoid the relapse. Yes, it might mean that you would have to give up some of those "friends" that you are accustomed to "hanging out" with, because they drink and could trigger a craving — and a relapse. It is not easy to give up the familiar. I know that from personal experience. When I first got sober, all of my friends were drinkers, and it was hard to break away from them and the comfort they had been. In truth, however, I had to make the break if I were going to stay sober and live, because they represented a return to my powerlessness and my unmanageable life.

Basic — H.A.L.T.!

Many words can be used for "halt." For openers, there are stop, stymie, stump, block, stall. Or consider hamper, impede, handicap. In the case of this basic, we ask that you employ any of those actions to the acronym that represents major relapse triggers — **H**unger, **A**nger, **L**oneliness, **T**iredness.

For us alcoholics, when we get hungry, our blood-sugar level drops. We get tired, and then we look for a drink to pick us up. Stop this relapse trigger in its place. Choose, instead, the safer, healthier, protein-rich foods, such as cheese, lean meat, or nuts.

Anger is one of the most common relapse triggers. According to Edith Packer, all emotions have a universal meaning. She was the first psychologist I've heard who talks about anger as a reaction to an injustice, whether that injustice is real or perceived. As a rule, you will alleviate your anger, which you probably have been taught is an inappropriate emotion, by indulging in your addiction, such as alcohol, drugs, food, or sex. Anger comprises two parts: what we think (mental) and what we do (energy) as a result of that anger. Block your anger. Change your thinking and do something to discharge the energy of the anger. Exercise is good, and so is sharing. Try them both. The primary relapse mode for alcoholics is to blame someone else for the injustice and to get angry enough to drink ourselves through the anger. Make it tough for you to do that by changing your thinking.

Loneliness is part of an alcoholic's makeup, because we alcoholics are loners at heart. Loneliness can create the craving, and the craving takes us down the wrong road. Stymie this relapse trigger immediately. Go to your support group, talk with someone in your alcohol-treatment program, call your sponsor, do anything to end the loneliness before you turn to alcohol. Unless we are in denial, we know that drinking makes the loneliness worse, not better.

Tiredness makes everything that is bad even worse. We can see no good solutions or alternatives to whatever we are experiencing. Vince Lombardi, the late, great coach of the Green Bay Packers said that, "Fatigue makes cowards of us all." He was right. When we are tired, our energy is sapped, and we take the easy road. We stop fighting. We hide out somewhere "safe." Alcoholics, I have observed, are generally high strung and have difficulty relaxing. We take our tiredness to new heights. We push the limits of our fatigue to accomplish something that might be better off left for another time. We replace our alcohol with our "workahol." We work too many hours, study too much, "hang out" too much. Sleep is for others, not for us. We have a hundred ways to increase our stress and bring on the old familiar craving. Thwart the craving brought on by tiredness. Break the cycle of workaholism. Take a nap. Go to a meeting of your support group. Read a book. Involve yourself in some creative activity.

All of the steps to practice this basic take some work. No one said that getting sober and maintaining that sobriety would be easy. If you practice these basics diligently, however, your sobriety will be in good hands. Get a picture of **H.A.L.T.!** clearly in your mind and keep it there. What does it look like? One of those forbidding gates in an old war movie? A octagonal sign with block letters? A barbed-wire fence between you and your hunger, anger, loneliness and tiredness? Make the symbol work for you.

Basic — Bring Your Body and Your Mind Will Follow

Bring your body, and your mind will follow. What that means is, if you, as an alcoholic, do the right things, such as go to meetings, get your rest, avoid the people, places, and things that lead to cravings, then your mind will fall into line. If you do the right thing, then right thinking and the right results will follow.

For instance, just showing up at meetings of your support group reinforces the principles that keep you sober. As one 12-step member said, "Don't drink, even if your ass falls off. If it falls off, put it in a paper bag and bring it to the meeting with you." The image might be gross, but it clearly illustrates the message: Go to the meetings, rather than drink. Bob E., a 12-step speaker from California, used to say, "We shall go to the meeting, the part of me that wants to go and the part of me that doesn't. You (my alcoholism, drug addiction, etc.) can sit in the corner and sulk, or you can come with me. Since you are attached to my head, I guess you are coming with me." Adopt this attitude, and you will find yourself sitting at a meeting, raising your hand and sharing, whether you want to, or not.

In the next chapter, we shall add some other basics that will help you to be firmly grounded in what it takes to achieve sobriety and to maintain it. Have faith. As we said in the beginning, we must know the basics before we can advance to the more difficult phases.

5
The Steps

When you accept the concept that your alcoholism is a disease, you have taken a big step toward your recovery from your addiction. Accepting the concept on its own is not enough, however. In his book The Rational Manager, the well-known corporate strategist Ben Treego puts great emphasis on defining what the problem is and what it is not, when trying to determine what a company's next strategic move might be, because it is a waste of time and effort to pursue any thought or situation that is not the problem. The same approach is true when dealing with your alcoholism.

In an earlier chapter we said that the disease of alcoholism — the problem of alcoholism — could be hereditary, or the condition could result from a combination of other factors. If we put this into a chart form, it would look like this:

Alcoholism or Other Addictions

What is the Problem	What is Not the Problem
Alcoholism (other addiction)	Stress Bad childhood Life difficulties

According to the authors of *Don't Help,* these three non-causes of alcoholism — stress, bad childhood, and life's difficulties — often are mistaken for the problem. Much popular literature is devoted to blaming poor parenting, life's traumas, and a host of other environmental conditions for alcoholism and drug addictions. If we are unable to control ourselves, the problem must lie outside of us, so the theory goes. As alcoholics, however, we must know that the alcohol, not the stress, not the rejection, not life's difficulties is the problem and make steps to change our thinking. The steps that I present within this book are based upon the 12 steps in Alcoholics Anonymous. I present them as one alcoholic to another, because there are only the two of us present at this particular moment.

❶ Step One

Admit that you are powerless over alcohol,
and that your life has become unmanageable.

As Father Martin, the well-known recovery speaker says in his book *Chalk Talk,* "What causes the problem is the problem." For the alcoholic, the problems are powerlessness and unmanageability. Our alcoholism renders us impotent in our battle over our addiction, and the resulting powerlessness swallows us in a life that becomes completely unmanageable. Step One occurs when you accept the disease of alcoholism and identify the problems that result from your alcoholism. When you have admitted to yourself that your life has become unmanageable, you are ready to take step two.

❷ Step Two

Come to believe that a Power greater than you can restore your freedom from the addiction and the sanity that accompanies the freedom.

When I entered one program, they told me that I could invent my own God. How foolish, I thought. How could I possibly invent my own "God"? They told me that my God could be understanding and accept me in spite of my alcoholism, or my God could be judgmental and indifferent. All I needed, they said, was an open mind and the willingness to try. So, I began to look for this "God" of mine. Eventually, I found my God, and with that discovery came help in dealing with my addiction.

What this amounted to was, that I believed in someone, something outside of myself. I acknowledged that I could not handle my addiction on my own. For some of my clients and others I have known, that power lies with "the group." For others, it's a "force." For still others, it's the God of organized religion. How you define your "God" is not important. What is important is, that the Higher Power lies somewhere outside of you, and you can give it definition.

What Columbus Knew About Faith

The story goes that on his first voyage across the Atlantic, Columbus instructed a person in the first boat to hold a lantern, in case one of the boats fell off the end of the world. It was the generally held opinion that the world was flat, and that if one traveled too far, one would fall off the earth. Columbus, however, believed that the world was round, although he didn't have faith that it was round. On his next trip across the Atlantic, Columbus didn't bother to have someone in the first boat hold the lantern because he had faith, gained from his first exploration, that the world was round, and that none of the boats would fall off, no matter how far they traveled.

Consider yourself like Columbus exploring the newness of your own world. First comes the belief that there is a power greater than you. Then comes the faith that this power can help you deal with your addiction to alcohol, or any other addiction.

Step Two is the turning point, the point at which you say that it is insane for you to think, much less believe, that you can ever take "just one drink." You know that alcoholism is a disease, that you are powerless over the disease, and that the disease makes your life unmanageable. Yet, you still think you can pick up that first drink. Remember the story of Bill Wilson, who picked up the first scotch and soda and found himself days later at the end of a binge? It is insane for you to believe that you can take the first drink and not lose control. Step Two, accepting the reality and the presence of a Higher Power, turns insane thoughts to sane ones that keep you from taking that drink.

Wilson tells that when he experienced his Higher Power, the room lit up. He asked for a sign that there truly was a God, and the room lit up. You probably will not experience a blinding flash of light. Your spiritual experience is more likely to be of the intellectual, educational variety, rather than a dramatic, physical sign. Psychologist William James says that this educational/spiritual experience will affect your behavior, and that, generally, others will notice the difference before you do.

Combine Step One, accepting a Higher Power in your life, with Step Two, dealing with the insanity of thinking that you can take the first drink, and move on to Step Three.

❸ Step Three

Give your life and your will over to the
care of God as you understand him.

When Fred entered AA, they told him that either God was God, or he was God. If God was God, then Fred should get out of the way and let God be God. Fred couldn't even run his own life, so how could he run the universe? The best thing for him to do, they said, was to resign from the God job. In other words, he had been unable to make his life better, so he should put his life and his will in the hands of his God and let life get better. The phrase in AA is, "Let go and let God," which ties together the thoughts of Step Three in five words.

This is a difficult concept to wrap your mind around, this belief that if you don't try to control things that are outside of your control and let those things go to your God, you will gain control. How can one give up control and gain it? The notion contradicts nearly every practical experience that we have had since childhood. Still, I can assure you, from personal experience, that it works.

In a meeting during one of his "doubting" phases, which you will experience during your recovery, just as I have, Fred thought the idea of letting go, of letting some "mythical" force handle his problem with alcohol, was ridiculous. He could see no rational basis for the idea. So he called a friend, a psychologist, and asked him to explain this if, in fact, he could. The psychologist told Fred that it works because Fred would no longer be focusing on the outcome of the situation or holding onto the idea that he can "handle this." M. Scott Peck, in *The Road Less Traveled,* writes that if a principle is true spiritually, then it also is true on a lower level psychologically.

The form you give the Higher Power in your life is not important. It is important, however, that you give your life and your will over to your God because, as you can see by the debris of failed relationships and jobs and the tenuous stability of your life, you have not been all that great in the God business. You will be amazed at how much stress is removed from your life when you no longer try to run the universe.

❹ Step Four

*Make a probing, courageous
moral inventory of yourself.*

Taking a serious, deep look at what motivates us, what we are trying to hide, what grows the warts on our character is nothing to fear. Yes, you might not like what you discover about yourself. You might even be repulsed by what you learn. But there is a simple truth to be gained in the exercise. Bill Wilson compares the problem with addiction to character defects, which has to do with our obsession with the source of our addiction. When we acknowledge and repair the defects in our character (lying, denying, blaming, etc.), we also eliminate the obsession. When we clean away the debris of our past and repair the flaws that keep us from living the day in its best form, we open our minds to that Higher Power. When we are free of the baggage of the past, our true spirituality can surface. In short, your spirituality cannot surface from under the ton of garbage that you carry with you in your defective character.

Fear is at the cornerstone of our defects. We fear what is being taken away from us as we move away from our addiction to a more spiritual existence. We fear what will happen if we do not get what we want. Rather than examining this fear, we employ our character defects to manipulate our world so that we can feel "safe."

According to Wilson, we humans have four basic instincts or drives — sex, security, prestige, and social contact. When any one of these is missing from our life, we experience distress. These instincts are a normal and natural part of life. When our fear gains ground, we let our instincts run wild, and we manipulate our environment to satisfy our instincts, rather than embracing the spirituality. Do not confuse spirituality with church attendance. Attending a church might help you, but understanding and accepting the part of you that reaches for and touches your God is what we seek. So long as you feed your fear and hold your spirituality at bay, your spiritual growth will be stunted. When you put your spiritual growth first, then you will be able to experience and to maintain sobriety. Taking Step Four is a way to bring yourself back into alignment with the true nature of your "self."

How to Do Step Four

Divide a piece of paper into four sections. Title the section on the left *The Events*. Title the section on the right *The Effects*. The two lower sections should be titled *The Instincts It Affected* and *The Character Defects*. Begin with *The Events* and write the events/actions that make you feel bad. Begin each statement with "I," and write as many statements as you need to complete your inventory. For example:

The Events	The Effects
1. I cheated on my wife . . . (husband, boyfriend, girlfriend).	My wife had a nervous breakdown.
2. I wrecked the car.	I got my third drunk-driving conviction.
3. I stole from my employer.	He went bankrupt.
4. I hurt someone I love by getting drunk.	They lost trust in me.

The Instincts It Affected	The Character Defects
1. Sex	1. Selfishness
2. Security	2. Resentment/fear
3. Prestige	3. Resentment/fear
4. Social contact	4. Pride

Complete this part of Step Four before you proceed to the next part. Be honest in your statements. Remember what we said about honesty in earlier chapters? This is an important time to be honest. Complete all responses in this section before you move on to the third part of Step Four.

The Events	The Effects
1. _____	_____
_____	_____
_____	_____
2. _____	_____
_____	_____
_____	_____
3. _____	_____
_____	_____
_____	_____
4. _____	_____
_____	_____
_____	_____

When you have completed your statements, take a look at the effects of the events/actions. What happened as a result of your cheating on your wife? What happened as a result of your wrecking the car? What happened as a result of your theft? Make complete statements about what resulted from the various events.

Which instinct did the event affect? More than one instinct can be involved because our lives are complex. They are not "this or that," or "either/or." Again, complete this section before you proceed to the next part.

When you have completed the third section, take a good look at your behavior and how it affected your world. Write which character defect(s) made it possible for you to engage in the event.

The Instincts It Affected	The Character Defects
1. _____	1. _____
_____	_____
2. _____	2. _____
_____	_____
3. _____	3. _____
_____	_____
4. _____	4. _____
_____	_____

When you have completed all sections, take a moment to review the entire page. Let the honesty of your words sink into your consciousness. The inventory of your character defects should be fairly clear. This is who you have been. It is not who you want to be. It is not who you will be as you begin to repair your character defects.

❺ Step Five

Admit to your God, to yourself, and to another person, the true nature of your wrongs.

In this step, you are encouraged to admit to your God, to yourself, and to another human being what you did, to whom, or what you did it to, and what happened as a result of your actions. Basically, you would be saying out loud what you have recorded in Step Four. In AA, the alcoholic has a sponsor, someone who shows the new member the ropes of the organization and someone with whom the new member can talk. For you, your confessor might be a good friend, or a nonjudgmental family member. What you are looking for is someone who can help you to more clearly understand your feelings and motivation. For instance, you might have thought that you were experiencing self-pity, when, in reality, you were experiencing resentment. Such a person in your life would help you to deal with the true nature of your situation.

By acknowledging and sharing the defects in your character out loud with another person, you will experience the full benefit of Step Five. Many of the alcoholics with whom I have worked reported feeling a new sense of relief. The guilt and the remorse they had been dragging around for years seemed to disappear.

A word of caution. Don't worry about making a "perfect" Step Five. Perfection is not your goal; starting the process and doing the best that you can is the goal.

Think About It, Do It:
The Order of the Steps

As my old mentor, Jesse Lair, used to say, "The steps go like this: First step, think about it, do it. Second step, think about it. Third step, turn it over (in your mind) and do it. Fourth step, take your inventory and think about it. Fifth step, talk (do it)." The steps are designed to make you think, to reflect upon your actions and then to take action.

❻ Step Six

Be prepared to have your God remove
the defects in your character.

This is a thinking step. It requires no action. This step requires only that you be ready to accept the change in thinking and understanding, and that you not fear it.

Fear itself was one of my major character defects. It kept me from knowing fulfilling relationships. Fear kept me from achieving my potential on the job or in any situation in which I was required to fully engage myself. Fear consumed my thoughts with every action in which I might have to invest myself, or to risk, or to trust. When I finally accepted that fear kept me from having a full and rewarding life, I asked Carl, another of my mentors, what I should do. "Find a quiet place and prepare yourself spiritually for what is to come," he told me. So, I went to a park and began my preparation.

❼ Step Seven

Humbly ask your God to
remove your shortcomings.

This step requires action. What kind of God have you created for yourself? What or who is your Higher Power? The same power that relieved your alcoholism will take away your character flaws, if you allow that to happen. Step Seven also is a humbling step. You probably will find it difficult to honestly admit that you have any flaws, much less identify them and ask for some unseen being to help repair them. The bottom line is, you do have character flaws, and these flaws keep you from achieving and maintaining sobriety.

When I went to my "quiet place," as Carl suggested, it was spring, and leaves were budding. I surrendered my defect of fear, just as I had surrendered my alcoholism. I truthfully admitted my defect and asked my God to remove my fear. There was no bolt of lightning. No shaking of the earth. I did, however, experience a warmth from the sun that reached deeply into my body and a release and a sense of peace that reached as deeply.

I offer two suggestions to make this step work for you. One, act as if the character flaw has been removed. I'm sure that you have heard the phrase "Fake it 'til you make it." This practice works in nearly every situation, not just with character flaws or alcoholism. This is the intellectual version of "dress for success." When you engage yourself in doing the "right thing," the "right thinking" will follow. Two, if you cannot remove a defect by acting as if you have, then pray for its removal. If you are put off by "prayer," think of this as sending off your intense desire for this defect to be removed to your God, whose job is to help you put your life right. You decided to give over these problems to your God in Step Three. Keep your eye on the step in front of you and keep climbing the steps.

You might desire to reach back to the "old you" when your character defects are gone, because that person is familiar and comfortable. In a way, I was afraid of what life would be like without fear. Nevertheless, I was prepared to have the flaw removed and to live without fear. When you are prepared to have your character defects removed, and you humbly ask to have them removed, you will be less attracted to your old ways.

Please keep in mind that you occasionally might have to return to Step Seven. Fear rises in me from time to time, but knowing about Step Seven and having experienced it gives me a sense of power over my fear. I return to Step Seven and gain control over my fear.

❽ Step Eight

*List all whom you have harmed and be
willing to make amends with all of them.*

"I know who I have harmed. I don't have to make any list," you protest. The physical act of writing this list helps you to come to terms with your defects and to let them go. The act requires that you once again consider what you have done. It requires that you confront the unpleasant side of your actions and to accept the responsibility for making things right between you and that person. If you need help in starting, go back to Step Four for some clues. You might even discover other names that should be added to your list.

Notice that this step asks only that you be willing to make amends to those whom you have harmed. I had a long list of people on the exercise in Step Four. My parents. A former girlfriend. A whole lot of other people I can't mention. "Reflect on that list," Carl told me. Again, I went to the park. I thought of all the people I had harmed, and I thought about the idea of being willing to make amends. All I did was think and allow my mind to explore the concept of making amends to these people. I felt a release and a lightness of spirit.

❾ Step Nine

*Make amends to those you have harmed,
unless to do so would injure them or others.*

This is a tough step. You must carefully decide how to make amends and whether to do so would injure the person in some other way or injure someone else. Making amends has little value if, in so doing, you create greater injury or spread the injury farther than it had spread in the first place. One such area is marital infidelity. This issue weighs heavily on many alcoholics, because it is such a sensitive one. Telling your spouse about your transgression might do more harm than would making amends. Or failing to make amends, only to have the spouse find out through some other means later, could cause more hurt. It truly is an issue that you will need to turn over to your High Power for guidance. In any event, you should not use the possibility of having someone get angry with you become an excuse for you not to make amends. The step does not say "Make amends, except when to do so would injure you."

Make amends as soon as you can. Don't put it off. It's like diving into water that you know is going to be cold. Putting off the dive does not make the water warmer; it just makes the dive harder to get through. Yes, the person with whom you want to make amends may tell you off, or refuse to speak to you. Rejection is not easy to take in the best of circumstances, but accept the fact that the water may be darn cold, inky black, and full of sharks, and dive in. When your head appears above water again, you will float. On the other hand, that person just might be waiting for you to make things right between you. No matter what the reaction might be, you must go forward.

After I had thought through the idea of making amends, I put aside my fear and embraced the need to set things right. Almost everyone was positive in the response to me. Most said I had not been as bad as I thought I had been. Others were just understanding. In some cases, I made amends in person. In others, I wrote to the person I had harmed, because I believed that a face-to-face encounter would have made matters worse. A friend of mine, upon the urging of a woman who was in 12-step recovery and en-couraged him to make amends, wrote to his ex-wife. At first, he thought the idea was a stupid one. The divorce was a stormy one, and his wife had been exceedingly angry about the break-up of the marriage. Nevertheless, he wrote the letter. He expected a letter of rage in reply, but, to his surprise, his ex-wife thanked him for his letter.

Whether things work out well, or whether nothing good happens, the goal of making amends, in whatever form that takes, is to begin your healing, not necessarily to repair a damaged relationship. You must first heal yourself.

Making restitution for monetary debts is part of mak-ing amends. If you owe your family back child-support, pay it. If you reneged on a debt, pay it. If you "appropriated" goods that were not yours, pay for them. This is your op-portunity to right a wrong — a wrong of your making.

You might be wondering why, if alcoholism is a dis-ease, you should have to do anything. You are not responsi-ble for the disease; however, you are responsible for overcoming the disease and achieving good health physi-cally, mentally, and spiritually. You must make amends in order to complete your journey to sobriety and to a life that is free from your alcoholism and your character defects.

6

The Maintenance Steps

⑩ Step Ten

Continue to take personal inventory,
and when you are wrong, promptly admit it.

The final three steps are called the maintenance steps because they ask you to renew your acquaintance with Step Four through Step Nine, the working steps, which help you to keep moving toward your journey's end — sobriety and good health.

Step Ten asks that you keep your personal inventory current. The "wrong" the step speaks of is the character defect that got out of hand and resulted in untoward behavior. For instance, you are fearful of giving a presentation. As a result of your fear, you spoke unjustly to someone, or blew your top and unloaded on the whole group. Drop back to Step Four and look deep into your heart and soul to, once again, bring your defects to mind. Examine the defects carefully and completely and own them. Move to Step Five and admit your wrongs to yourself, to your God, and to someone you trust. Prepare yourself to let go and let God, in Step Six, then move on to Step Seven in which you ask your God to remove the character flaw that caused you to behave so poorly. Step Eight asks you to make a list of the people you harmed in your latest demonstration of your defective character.

It is important to note here that engaging in any Twelve Step program is not a matter of checking off each step as you complete it. To the contrary, my friend. You aren't building a model airplane or a shed in which the directions are clear and knowable. You are rebuilding your life. Working one's way back to sobriety and the freedom from addiction is a continual assessment and reassessment of your spiritual health. You might have to return to Step Three, deciding to give your life over to a Higher Power, because you think you are back in the God business. Or you might even have to return to Step One and reaffirm your powerlessness over alcohol and that your life has once again become unmanageable. Eventually, you will more fully understand what is happening in your life and reach for the Step that will put you back on track.

Bill Wilson, in the book *Twelve Steps and Twelve Traditions,* says that there are three ways to do Step 10 so that it benefits you. One way is to make a spot check of your behavior throughout the day, whenever the warning light is blinking in the back of your mind. Another way is to do an inventory at the end of the day, say, before you go to sleep. The third way is to review at some specific point in the day, perhaps at lunch, what you did in the morning and how you would do it differently if you could do it all over again. By making this Step a regular part of each day, you can more effectively work on your shortcomings and bring about real change in your life. Step Ten is a regular part of my days, and I recommend the ritual to you.

⑪ Step Eleven

Seek, through prayer and meditation, to improve your conscious contact with your God, and pray for the knowledge of your God's will and the power to carry it out.

Step Eleven is an expansion of Step Three, which asks that you give your life and your will over to your Higher Power. In this case, we can call prayer a conversation with God and meditation, the energy-giving practice of dwelling on the good and the strong that enables us to carry out God's will. In other words, now that you have repaired your character by employing Step Four through Step Nine, you can more confidently and humbly allow the grace of God to enter your life. As Bob E. (a seminar leader and AA speaker) says, "I thought God's will for me was to be 20y years sober and celibate, working in a men's halfway house, washing dishes, talking about gratitude. Well, it doesn't have to be that way." Your understanding of the process might reveal itself that way, as a "hunch" or the occasional brainstorm, but by being true to the Twelve Steps, inspiration will begin to replace the haphazard flashes of insight. When you are upset, for instance, you will pause, ask for guidance, and calmly reflect upon your situation. Calmness is a key ingredient. In many of the world's religions, calmness is considered an essential part of spirituality, because calmness allows you to think clearly, to hear the voice of your God, and to receive the help you have requested. Through my study of Aikido (a martial art), I have learned that when I am relaxed, I am far better able to institute a reasonable, positive and constructive course of action. When I know the will of my God, I can then pray for the power to follow through by processing Step Four through Step Nine again. This re-examination of the steps does not mean that you will have to do something that will make you uncomfortable or something that you might very well hate (such as Bob's example); rather, you will realize that it is in your best interest to follow a particular course of action.

In his audiotape program *The Psychology of Achievement,* Brian Tracy gives a few examples of what it is like to access a Higher Power. One, called the "blinding flash of the obvious," involves examining a problem or suddenly realizing the solution to a problem. Michael Faraday, the father of the modern solid-state theory, realized the solution to a problem in a dream. He woke up, went to his laboratory, and developed the basics for the solid-state theory of conductivity. He said the solution came to him in its entirety, complete, and without any improvement needed.

Another way to know whether a Higher Power is contacting us is through chance encounters with other people. Carl Jung, the psychiatrist and psychologist who gave us theories about what goes on in our unconscious self, called these encounters "synchronicity," a kind of happy meshing of events. Let's say that you are thinking through an especially difficult situation. You can't quite find a path through the maze. Suddenly, and unexpectedly, someone comes along with the answer you need to solve your dilemma. That person probably won't even know the impact that his or her words or actions had upon you and your situation. Or, perhaps, you read an article in a magazine or newspaper, or see a television show, and some word, or scene, or expression brings to light a solution to your problem. Synchronicity.

In AA, such coincidences are described as, "the hand of God acting anonymously." Twelve-step programs are among the few places in which such happy coincidences are considered common occurrences. These coincidences are believed to be the result of letting go, as emphasized in Step Three and Step Eleven. I recall a sychronistic event in my life that occurred when I had been in recovery only a few years. I went out to start my car. The battery was dead. In haste, and probably in anger, I left the car — and locked my keys inside. While I was in this turmoil, I kept thinking about my sponsor and of Step Three, and that the program I was in was a crock of you-know-what, and other such thoughts. I thought I could at least get my landlady to let me in to call someone. She wasn't home. Exasperated, I walked over to a pizza place and asked a boy, who was about 16, if he had a hanger I could use. No, no hanger, but he could open the car without one. Partly to appease him and partly because I had nothing to lose, we went to my car. As we were walking toward the car, a guy dressed like a hippie started to pass me on the sidewalk. He was carrying hangers. Not hangers with clothes on them, or hangers in a box. Just hangers. I explained my situation and asked for a hanger. "Wow," says the guy, "It's not everyday you run into someone carrying hangers when you need one." This was indeed a fortuitous meshing of events. The rest, as "they" say, is history. I had a hanger, I opened my car and, eventually, I got my car started.

You can call this coincidence if you want, but I think it was more than that. To paraphrase Shakespeare in *Hamlet,* there are more things in heaven and earth than are dreamt of in our philosophies. Of course, I am not the only person who has experienced events such as this. Practicing the 12 steps, however, does seem to make one more aware of such events when they unfold.

Another way to experience Step 11 is to listen to your intuition. We often call this the "still, small voice within," your God finding an avenue of communication that reaches you. Buddha talked about the God within. And an old African proverb states, "If there is no enemy within, the enemy without can do you no harm." Tapping into this intuition, listening to this still, small voice to guide you, is what some philosophers call the "higher mind." By the time someone reaches this step, he or she is inner directed and looking for guidance from within. Gandhi would sit from Friday to Sunday in silence. He would meditate and look inward for direction. Gandhi wasn't addicted to alcohol, but he took to heart the principles we know in Step 11.

I offer a note of caution in engaging in this step. Your intuition should never violate the rules of common sense. Ayn Rand, the philosopher and novelist, said that when your emotions and logic contradict, you should go with your logic. In this case, you can substitute intuition for emotion. For instance, if you are sober for two months, and your intuition tells you to go hang out with your coke-snorting friends, but your logic tells you that this would be a dangerous move, listen to your logic. If you have been at your job for 10 years and a moment of bravado rising from six months of sobriety prompts you to quit your job, listen for your voice of logic. Consider what would result from such an impulsive move.

This is why the *Twelve and Twelve** stresses that going it alone in spiritual matters is dangerous. To emphasize this truth, Bob E. tells how after he had been sober for a few years, he asked a spiritual woman in the program what meditation was. "Bobby," she said, "that's easy. Just close your eyes and listen to the still, small voice within." "Which one?" Bobby asked. "I've got about six of them, and they've all got opinions on something." It might seem like you have many voices talking to you, but, in reality, you have only one voice that speaks in logic. Using that truth as a basis, I offer two strong pieces of advice: Use your logic as a guide and a ground, and two, if you still wonder about the direction you are about to undertake, talk with someone you trust. If you do both of these, you will be less likely to run into problems.

⑫ Step Twelve

Having experienced a spiritual awakening as a result of practicing the principles of these 12 steps, help other alcoholics, and continue to practice the principles in all our affairs.

Step 12 is the reminder that a 12-step recovery program is, or should be, a way of life. Steps Four through Nine are the backbone of the program, and consistent practice of them is necessary in every part of your life, not just in the meeting rooms where you participate in the program. If you are to achieve sobriety and maintain it, then the steps must become a integral part of your life, each day, every

---

*The book *Twelve Steps and Twelve Traditions* is a companion to the *Big Book.*

day. We alcoholics, you and I, must keep the principles clearly in our minds and in our actions.

What about helping other alcoholics? Isn't it a bit presumptuous for the alcoholic to try to help another alcoholic? In days gone by, it was common for recovering alcoholics to make "12-Step" house calls, in which one alcoholic would go to the house of another alcoholic to help that person avoid a return to the bottle. Now, however, alcoholics generally are detoxified in a hospital, and few alcoholics make house calls. Working with another alcoholic is, nevertheless, a beneficial part of your recovery. Dr. Bob, the cofounder of AA, says, "Whenever I feel like drinking, nothing works to keep me from drinking like intensive work with another alcoholic. Or, as we say in 12-step treatment, "To get it, you have to give it away."

Bill McD. understood what it meant to give it away. Bill was an African-American who stood about 6 foot 5 and weighed about 280 pounds. His frame filled a doorway; his voice filled a room. For many years, Bill carried the message to alcoholics in prison. Some inmates came to meetings because they had to, others came and were bored. But always one or two inmates came to Bill and his small band of sober, recovering alcoholics to talk about the what had been said in the meeting. The enthusiasm of those few always bolstered Bill and his crew.

Step Twelve also has to do with exceeding one's self-centeredness, or selfishness, if you will. The compulsion and the obsession to satisfy your need to drink are about you. Working with another alcoholic, or anyone in need, for that matter, takes you outside of yourself. As a result of focusing your attention on someone else, whatever was triggering your compulsion or obsession becomes a secondary focus, if it has any focus at all.

We have long known that volunteer work and high self-esteem walk hand in hand. AA members, for example, are encouraged to join the hospitals and institutions group in your home group that matches volunteers to community needs. It will, however, be necessary for you to have been sober for at least 90 days before you sign up for this opportunity. It is important that only sober people carry the message to other alcoholics.

What also is true about volunteering is, that when you teach something, a craft, a skill, whatever, you learn still more about that topic. Sharing your abilities with others helps you to understand just how much you know, which boosts your feeling of self-worth and your knowledge. The more seminars I teach, the better I get at what I am doing. This is true for all of us.

If you could work with your local hospital, for instance, to bring a 12-step meeting into the hospital, you not only will be helping the alcoholics in treatment, but you also will benefit from the experience. You gain a better understanding of what you are doing as a recovering alcoholic, and the appreciation of those you help will improve your self-perception. No matter how lousy you feel about yourself when you start your volunteer work, the longer you work at it, the better you will feel about yourself. In AA they say, "If you have a problem, go find another alcoholic to help, and you will have half a problem." So, let this step remind you, once again, you are not on your own. You have a Higher Power to help you, and you have the opportunity to help yourself as you help someone else.

Make the Steps Part of Your Life

By now you have read through or been associated with at least one 12-step program, one of the most powerful forms of therapy. Now, take those steps to heart and make them a part of your life. If you follow the suggestions for taking these steps, your life will begin to change. They will be little changes at first, but the changes will continue and grow as you practice the steps and make them an integral part of your life.

Much of what has been written about breaking one's addiction doesn't work. I know that this program works. It changed my life, and it has changed the lives of hundreds of alcoholics with whom I have worked. Work is the key. You will have to work and to practice and to reassess your progress and, maybe, even start over again. Few things in life that are truly beneficial can be accomplished without work — diligent, continuous, sometimes spirit-testing work. Sobriety is one of those things.

7
The Meetings

Just as 12-step programs abound, so do group sessions that are designed to help people like us, those who need to know that we are not alone in our struggle. I am partial to the Alcoholics Anonymous meetings for those who are in early recovery because they embrace you at whatever level you happen to be in your journey toward continued sobriety. They also involve you in the whole of the process, not just the "you" in the process. They ask you to take responsibility not only for your sobriety, but also your place in the health of the group and to reach outside of yourself.

AA, which comprises almost two million members in the United States, along with its Narcotics Anonymous and Alanon (the 12-step program for relatives and friends of alcoholics) is the oldest and probably the largest fellowship of its kind in the world. It includes people from all walks of life, "from Park Avenue to park bench," as one prominent AA speaker says. From plumbers to scientists and everything between and beside them. At any one AA meeting you might find a businesswoman in a Chanel suit, a biker, a grandmother, a rapper, a priest. This diversity, the blending of personalities and experiences makes these meetings powerful spiritual soup to nourish your soul, as you work your way toward sobriety.

The AA program has more than one kind of meeting, another kind of diversity that reinforces your strengths, asks you to grow in your journey and helps you to learn still more about yourself and what it will take to achieve your goal. Here is an overview of the AA program.

Speaker Meetings

The "speaker meeting" is the most commonly known among outsiders. You've seen it depicted in movies and television shows. You know, the smoke-filled room, with a person at the podium telling about his or her battle with alcoholism. Each speaker's story relates to what the person experienced during their active addiction, how recovery began and what the person experiences currently. Not all speakers conform to this exact format, but most do.

Speaker meetings are particularly valuable if you follow one simple but vital rule: identify with what the speaker is saying, don't compare yourself with the person. You are no better or worse than the person who is speaking; you are just different, but still very much the same.

Identify, Don't Compare

I cannot stress strongly enough the idea that it is important for you to concentrate on listening for and opening your mind to the words that will help you. If your mind is open, your God will find a way to speak to you. The therapy that rises from these meetings is powerful.

The most obvious level of identification lies in what the speakers have done. For example, we have two speakers. The first is a tough biker type, with long hair, beard, and tattoos everywhere. He talks about being in trouble with the law, about being arrested, going to jail, and other experiences better left unrepeated. Then he gets into what his life is like now: a life of sobriety, of helping others, and of kindness and love. The second speaker is an elderly man, a grandfatherly sort of guy. He tells how he was a closet drinker, the kind who never left home to tie one on. Then he talks about what his life is like. If you heard nothing except the introductory stories, you would think that these two men had nothing in common. But there always is "the rest of the story," the part of the story that deals with the here and the now. Each speaker went from telling about the details of the alcoholism to relating the more painful inside stuff. The loneliness. The isolation. The self-hatred for what happened as a result of the drinking. The two who are individuals in their physical presence become one in their common experiences, and the isolation and the loneliness ease a little. If you attend these meetings often enough, you will hear your story, or familiar pieces of your story, and say to yourself, "Hey! If he can do it, I can do it!"

Raymond told about attending a 12-step meeting in which John S., a tall, lean, good-looking fellow in his late thirties, talked about his days of being the town drunk — and about being confined to a wheelchair because he had alcoholic neuropathy. (He had been in Stage 3 deterioration.) Raymond took heart and courage from John's message and told himself that if John, who now stood to make his remarks, could make it back from hell, then so could he. That Raymond is sober and can talk about his experience now is the true power of the 12-step recovery. The power begins to grow when one alcoholic identifies with another and finds new resolve, new courage.

Home Group

The speaker meeting is, for most people, the group you join, which is called your "home group." You attend your home group every week, and you make yourself part of the home by setting up chairs, making coffee, putting out the literature, or maybe even greeting people as they come into the room. I have yet to meet anyone who experienced a really solid home group who failed to get sober.

To join a home group, you simply sign up with the secretary of the group by giving your sobriety date. If the secretary is not readily obvious, just ask whom you should see about joining the group. The key here is to come back, week after week. Your comfort level will grow. Your knowledge of the members in your home group will grow. You will gain inner peace and strength.

Business Meeting

Business meetings are announced before the speaker meeting begins. The business meeting is an extension of the speaker meeting. You gather after the speaker meeting for 15 to 20 minutes to discuss various AA activities and your home group.

There is room for growth here, too. When you have achieved a consistent sobriety and have attended several business meetings with your home group, you could become an intergroup representative. The intergroup is the governing body of AA and comprises only members.

Regardless of whether you aspire to a broader involvement in the AA meetings, you should become an active participant in your home group. Come early, stay late. At least 30 minutes. Do whatever is necessary to set up and to clean up. Don't worry about what others are doing; do what is necessary for you to achieve your goal. Understand that AA is a "selfish" program. Your sobriety comes first, before everything else. This thought should be ever present in your mind. Think of it this way: There is good selfishness and bad selfishness. Bad selfishness might be your lying or being dishonest to get your way in order for you to continue drinking. Good selfishness puts your recovery first. Be selfish enough to allow your time at the meetings to satisfy your needs.

Home Group and More

The home group invites in speakers from other home groups and *vice versa*. This exchange is called a "commitment." When you participate in a commitment, you tell your story, just as you did in your home group. Generally, three AA members bring the commitment, although more can go along for moral support. When you can talk about your journey with a new group, not just the home group, your resolve grows. The words, spoken aloud in a new setting, give you renewed strength. You probably won't be ready to speak in the early days, but keep the possibility of speaking in the forefront of your mind, because when you go out on a commitment, you will begin to truly understand the power that lies within you.

Beyond your Home Group

Early in your sobriety, it is helpful to attend other speaker meetings for the additional exposure. The objective is to maintain your link with others who are working their way to continued sobriety between meetings of your home group. Again, go early and stay late, maybe 15 minutes or

so. Make a variety of speaker meetings part of your reper-
toire. They will keep you moving toward your goal of lasting sobriety and good health.

Discussion Meeting

A member described a discussion meeting as a combination of group therapy and a town meeting. Usually, the
meeting has a topic, such as people, places, things, or the
first step. Participants raise their hands when they wish to
enter the discussion, and the discussion can become very
lively. Again, the key is to identify with what is being said,
not to compare your attitudes, your recovery with that of
another. One of the first things that people who join AA
learn is, that if I am pointing my finger at someone and telling that person what he "should" do, I have three fingers
pointing right back at me. You attend these meetings to focus on the similarities and to share experiences, strength
and hope with one another.

In these meetings, just as in nearly every other place in
your life, you will encounter someone who "knows it all."
These experts are everywhere. The truth is, while I am an
expert in my own recovery, I can't tell you how to go about
yours. No one can. I do offer suggestions in this book of
things that have worked for me. These things might not
work for you in quite the same way as they did for me.
You might have to make adjustments and vary the plan, but
the plan will work.

One way to keep these "experts" from confusing you
and to avoid the temptation to become an "expert" is to use
what counselors call "I" language. Begin your statements
with "I." "I feel . . ." "I think . . . " The "bleeding dea-
cons" (members in a 12-step program who impose them-

selves as authorities on how you should manage your life) exist. I mention them here so that you will be forewarned.

Remember that, basically, everyone at a meeting is there to share and not to give advice. Keep your attitude positive and moving forward by identifying with the strength of another and sharing yours with someone else.

Step Meeting

Step meetings are simply meetings that concentrate on one step. The best of them, from my perspective, are those that focus each meeting on a single step. The group reads through the entire step and then discusses it. The worst of these meetings, again from my perspective, are those that carry a step from one week to another. Your viewpoint might be different from mine, but what is important for you to know is that different groups manage their meetings in different ways. To help you gain the maximum benefit from your time with any group, visit several groups, and then stick with the one that meets your needs. Be selfish with your time and invest it where the meetings more completely meet your needs.

One other point to remember is that you don't have to wait for a group to reach step one again before you can participate. You begin the program where they are. You should have read through the twelve steps by the time you attend a Step Meeting, and you will have a general knowledge of the program. Don't let the fact that the group is not on Step One become an excuse for your not attending Step meetings.

Other Meetings

From a practical point of view, more than 80 percent of the meetings that you will attend fall into the categories of home group, speaker meetings, Discussion meetings and step meetings. The remainder fall into one of the categories below.

Big Book Meeting

The *Big Book* is like the Bible of the AA program and contains a variety of information on how to be successful in your journey and to maintain your success. The *Big Book* meetings are similar in format to step meetings in that someone reads a passage from the book, and a discussion follows. These meetings increase your knowledge of how the *Big Book* can help you.

Speaker/Discussion Meeting

In this type of meeting, the speaker talks for the first 30 minutes or so. Then the meeting is opened to allow participants to share and to identify with the speaker. Basically, this is a speaker meeting with a discussion.

Beginner's Meeting

In its best form, the beginner's meeting focuses on first-step issues. Members with long-term sobriety may attend, but they are encouraged to give the early sobriety members the chance to meet their needs first.

Double-Trouble Meeting

These meetings are for members who, in addition to their alcoholism, have a psychiatric illness. AA recognizes that you must deal with all of you, not just your alcoholism, in order to make things work.

Young People and Special-Interest Groups

In recent years, special-interest groups have sprung up. These have resulted from the increase in membership and the increase in the diversity of members. In its early years, from its founding in 1935 to the late 1940s, most of the AA members were over 40 years of age. The organization gained wider notice at the end of the 40s, when Jack Alexander wrote an article about AA for the Saturday Evening Post. Enrollment in AA increased substantially. Membership made small gains until the late 1970s, when the Baby Boomers began to enter AA. When that population and the population from the alcohol rehabilitation groups began to join AA, membership boomed and so did the special-interest groups. In fact, between 1978 and 1988, membership in AA doubled, and the median age dropped considerably.

The special needs and special interests began to sort themselves out. The group for young people, which began as a splinter group, if you will, has become a driving force in AA. By the year 2000, it will be part of the decision-making body in AA. Other special-interest meetings include meetings for bikers, couples, gays, free-thinkers, and professionals, just to name a few. You might find a meeting at the local college or near a large office complex, where workers meet at lunch. It doesn't matter what kind of meetings you attend, so long as the group meets your needs and you do attend the meetings regularly.

The objective in all of these meetings is to help you understand that you are not alone, that you don't have to meet the challenge alone, and that you can help to heal yourself by sharing with others in similar circumstances.

Whether you participate in an AA program or some other program is not important. The basics in this book will work for you if you work with them, regardless of what 12-step program you choose.

8
Feelings, Anyone?

Before we begin this chapter on feelings, let me give you some room to breathe, if you need it. We understand that alcoholics in early recovery frequently are too confused to deal with their feelings or to identify them. If the next few pages are confusing or too much for you to handle right now, read this section of the book after you have been sober a little longer. Recovery is a slow process. Don't try to hurry it or to force it. Remember to let recovery happen, not make it happen.

Once you understand the fundamentals of how recovery takes place, however, you have to start dealing with your feelings.

Feelings are key to nearly everything we do and everything that we are. Our relationships are based upon how we feel about the other person or persons and how we feel in the company of that person or those persons. How well we function on the job is, for instance, based upon how we feel about our environment, our coworkers, the attitude of those around us, the company's attitude toward its employees, and how we feel about ourselves in this environment. Our comfort at home is based, among other things, upon how we feel about our neighborhood, the amenities in our home, the amount of space that we have and whether home is a permanent or temporary location.

Feelings also pop up when we least expect them, and they often are triggered by events that we have long since relegated to some corner of our mind because we no longer wanted to deal with them, or because the events are too painful to recall.

How we deal with feelings can have a major impact on our lives. This information came to me very late in my recovery. I offer it to you now because our feelings play an essential role in our recovery. What exactly are feelings? Where do they come from? Why do we have them? Let's begin with what a feeling is. Dr. Edith Packer, in her audio tape *The Art of Introspection,* describes a feeling as a psychosomatic response to a thought, or a mind-body response to a thought. She calls a feeling an instantaneous value judgment. Ayn Rand says that emotions (feelings) are tools of cognition. Both are saying the same thing: Our feelings come from our thoughts. For example, if you are feeling a negative feeling, you are, in all probability, thinking negative thoughts. You could, just as easily, think positive thoughts and turn your feelings toward positive responses. Thinking creates feelings, and we can, to a large degree, choose how we are going to feel by adjusting our thinking.

We need feelings to help us accomplish our goals. In line with what I said above, negative feelings help us to accomplish negative goals; positive feelings help us to accomplish positive goals. Feelings mostly work in two directions, either moving us toward something that we like and admire, such as when we pursue someone we find especially attractive in some way, or moving us away from something that we hate or fear, such as broccoli or heights. To accomplish a goal, one needs to feel deeply about the subject and the outcome of the work put into accomplishing the goal.

As a matter of explanation, a goal need not be some lofty plan that will end in a major occurrence. A goal could be as simple as being on time to every appointment. Before you can accomplish that goal, however, you need to have strong feelings about being on time. If you are indifferent about being on time, you won't be on time to anything.

You don't have feelings, you say? Contrary to popular belief, people do not block feelings. You do not block feelings. What you do is block the perception or the evaluation of your situation. For instance, someone you thought was a trusted friend betrays your trust. At first, you consciously block your thoughts about this event. You can't look at the event because it is too painful or too confusing, and so you don't look at it. This conscious blocking is called suppression, which is one of two basic defense mechanisms. The other mechanism is repression and occurs when we have blocked our thoughts about what happened so vigorously and so completely that the blocking is unconscious and becomes habitual.

Perhaps you have repressed thoughts about how you were verbally abused as a child. At the time of the abuse, you became angry. Every verbal insult resulted in anger that seethed inside you. You consciously blocked (suppressed) the thoughts as a matter of self-preservation and the blocking became habit (repression). Years later, as an adult, the anger surges when someone yells at you or honks at you for failing to move forward when the traffic light turns green.

Because of your early childhood experiences (the "there" and the "then" in your life), you will react with anger to all similar events in the here and the now as if you still were there and then, still in your childhood.

Here is a six-step method that can help to bring about, in many cases, rapid improvement of such emotional symptoms.

Step One: Ask yourself what you are feeling at that moment. If, for instance, you were the person at the traffic signal who was "too stupid to know the difference between a red light and a green one," take a few minutes in a neutral setting, where you can think more clearly. Some place that does not hold the same possibility or memory of criticism. Ask yourself: What am I feeling?

The responses will vary. "I'm feeling anger! He didn't need to shout at me like that!" Am I feeling anything else? "I feel sad. Why can't people give me the benefit of the doubt like I do them?" Anything else? "Fear. I'm afraid that this road rage might have resulted in my being injured." If this had happened to me, I might have felt fear, along with depression and guilt, with anxiety, shame, and sadness tossed in for good measure.

Anger usually is accompanied by several emotions, such as fear or sadness or guilt. It is important, too, that you understand that there are no "right" or "wrong" feelings. There are only feelings, and they are yours. In the beginning of my recovery, I understood that there was no morality, no judgment of good or bad, attached to a feeling, because feelings are just that, feelings. But something was missing. Then I learned that every feeling has a meaning. When you learn what you are thinking, you understand the feeling. Then you can ask yourself whether the feeling is appropriate to the current situation.

Step Two: Why do I feel this way? After you determine what you are feeling, the next step is to find out what brought about the feeling. Feelings have universal meanings. Anger means, for instance, that someone, most likely you, has experienced an injustice. Rev. Martin Luther King Jr. and Gandhi are two examples of how anger can be used appropriately. Rev. King harnessed his anger about segregation to correct the injustice. Gandhi, just as peaceably, used his anger to correct the injustices brought about by English rule in India. The meaning of fear is you are physically or psychologically being threatened. Guilt says that you did something that was not worthy of you. Sadness comes from the loss of something or someone of value, and it is the signal that you need to replace it with something else of value.

Unfortunately, there is no one book in which you can look up the meaning of feelings. For one reason, there are too many feelings. Dr. Packer says we can experience several hundred feelings. A catalog of feelings certainly would benefit mankind, but, for the time being, we can assign meanings to the feelings we know. Dr. Packer suggests that you follow two simple rules. One, ask yourself, "If this feeling could talk, what would it say to me?" You might glibly answer, "You shouldn't have done that." Such a "cover-all" answer would, as we say in the program, be your disease talking back to you, giving you room to excuse yourself. If you think a little longer and more carefully about your actions, your words might tell you specifically how your action was not worthy of you. Usually, this technique yields results.

If, however, the words still have not come to you, Dr. Packer recommends asking yourself this question: What would someone else feel if they were in this situation? For instance, "What would my sponsor feel?" or "What would my best friend feel?" Stressful situations often produce feelings that we repress or deny. With careful introspection, however, we usually can define what we are feeling.

Step Three: Feelings are triggered by events. Find out what triggered yours. You must be specific about the origin of your feeling. Many people in the program talk about their pain, without tying it to a specific event. Their talk sounds like this: "A lot of pain has been coming up lately, and I have been dealing with some issues." However, when someone asks what brought about the pain, they reply, just as vaguely, "Oh, nothing specific. I am just in pain." Feelings begin somewhere. They don't just "happen." You might not consciously be aware of the event that triggered the pain, but you can be sure that a specific event triggered the feeling. The event could have occurred, and most likely did occur, in the case of alcoholics, well into the past, but an event today made the past come alive. Someone honking at you at the traffic signal, for instance, brought your past into the car with you.

Step Four: Ask yourself what you are really thinking. Feelings come from thoughts. What are you really thinking about the incident? We don't want to know what you think your sponsor thinks you should be thinking, or what you are "supposed" to be thinking, or what you might be thinking if you were sober longer. What are you really thinking about what happened at the traffic signal? Write down your thoughts in a notebook that is privately yours. Write whatever thoughts come into your mind about this particular incident. If you don't like to write, use a tape recorder. If you would rather talk to someone, talk with a good friend in a 12-step program or with a 12-step-oriented counselor. Or go to a meeting. There is something about sitting quietly in a meeting, with no phone ringing and nothing required of you, and reflecting on the incident with your Higher Power while you soak up the good feelings of the fellowship.

Your thinking might go something like this — "This isn't fair (injustice). If he really is mad at me, I might get hurt (fear). I wish I were more assertive (unworthiness). I'm no good. I thought sobriety was going to be better than this (sadness). What can I do? What can I do? (helplessness)." For starters, don't be ashamed of your feelings. They are your feelings, and you can't change them until you know them and own them. Bob E. had a favorite saying at meetings. He told us that if our neighbor talked to us as we talk to us, we wouldn't stand for it. He's right. Until we know what stirs those feelings, however, all we will do is to keep beating up on ourselves verbally.

Step Five: Look at the facts. This step might be the hardest of all. This step requires you to look at the facts of your situation and then, based upon the facts, not your feelings, draw your conclusion about the appropriateness of your feelings. In medicine, treatment of your illness depends upon your illness being properly diagnosed. The same holds true for the treatment of your illness. Addicts judge their lives by what they feel; successful people judge life by the facts. If your emotions and your logic contradict each other, go with your logic. This does not mean that your feelings are unimportant. To the contrary, your feelings are very important, but you should judge their validity in light of the facts associated with the situation. Are the thoughts that brought about the feelings appropriate to the situation?

In the example of your being verbally abused at the traffic signal, bring in all facts that are relevant to the situation. Was any real injustice done to you? Maybe the interstate was crowded and a mass of cars was backed up on the off ramp. There is much confusion and yelling. In reality, the driver was not yelling at you. He was just yelling. Do the facts indicate that you were doing anything wrong? No, you were traveling the speed limit and driving courteously. Does someone's rudeness in this confusion mean that your situation is hopeless, your sobriety useless? What do you know to be true about the particular event in your life? Sort carefully through the facts and keep the facts separate from the emotions.

Step Six: *Pull it all together.* In this step, we look at all of the rational components of the process and come up with new thoughts, based upon the facts as we know them. *Fact:* traffic was pretty messed up on the exit ramp, but I didn't do anything to contribute to that, except hold my place in line. *Fact:* The offensive driver was rude. His rudeness is his problem, not mine, and I am not going to make it my problem. *Fact:* What is happening in traffic has no bearing on your sobriety. The situation on the off-ramp does not change the importance of sobriety or its worth. You just were traveling on the interstate at the wrong time for this particular time and circumstances.

Father Joseph Martin, a prominent speaker in the field of alcoholism, narrates *Chalk Talk,* a film in which he describes one's recovery from alcoholism as an equation in which $E/I + AA = I/E$ (Emotions over Intellect plus Alcoholics Anonymous equals Intellect over Emotions). We could just as easily say emotions over intellect plus your faithful practice of a 12-step program equals intellect over emotions. The important thing to know here is, in the early stages of recovery, an alcoholic — you — will respond to reality, to concepts such as "a thing is a thing, and it is not something else." You should remember reading this concept, the Law of Identity, in Chapter Two. Alcoholic drinking is alcoholic drinking, no matter what you say from your alcoholism. So, you can live the problem (E/I), or you can live the solution (I/E).

As someone living in the solution, you might approach the verbal abuse by deciding that the weather and the traffic were enough to set off a verbal attack, even though the attack made you angry. The driver certainly should have behaved more responsibly, and you might have been a little more aware in such conditions, but was anger the best response from you?

Dr. Packer has devised a method of rating anger from one to 10, with 10 representing the greatest injustice and one the least. (Understand, right now, that your disease will not want you to do this.) I would rate anger in this situation as a two. This does not mean that it is unimportant; it means only that it should not be given more importance than it deserves. A two on the anger scale is not the same as a 10, regardless of what your disease says or wants you to believe.

Any of the other feelings that you might have felt in connection with this event can be evaluated just as clearly, and you can put to use the I/E part of the equation. If guilt is weighing you down, even though you have done nothing wrong, the guilt probably was triggered by some word or action that brought your past into the present. What do the facts of the situation tell you? If there are no facts to back up your feeling of guilt, decide to use the I/E approach. Enjoy your life. Talk about the event with your sponsor or in a meeting. Go out to eat after the meeting. Focus on the things in your life that you do have and can enjoy.

If you practice this technique on a regular basis and follow the guidelines contained in this chapter, you will achieve results that will surprise you. People from my seminars have come up to me years later to say how the technique has helped them to stay on course. The benefit of the technique is, however, proportional to the amount of practice — consistent, diligent practice — that you put into your sobriety.

Feelings Abound

We have talked a bit about anger, fear, sadness, and guilt, but life is full of other feelings, as well. A colleague of mine, a psychologist, once remarked that learning the meaning of feelings was one of the most valuable lessons in a recovery program. "There normally isn't any talk on the meanings of feelings," he told me. The fact that most programs do not deal with the meaning of feelings makes this section so significant.

Anxiety is a major feeling that imposes itself upon the alcoholic almost daily. Before I continue explaining anxiety, I offer a safety valve for you. If you are in a highly sensitized state and experience panic attacks, I recommend that you delay using this technique. It could confuse you, and we don't want you to make any needless side trips on your road to recovery. If, however, you are not experiencing panic attacks, forge ahead. This section will help you.

Anxiety amounts to you telling yourself that "I doubt myself." You doubt your ability to use your mind to solve the problems in your life. If you evaluate the situation that causes you anxiety as you evaluate the others, focusing on the facts of the situation, you will discover that your doubt rarely has basis in reality. Just being able to think that your self-doubt has no basis in fact and that engaging in it results in misplaced energy are powerful thoughts.

Following right behind anxiety is depression. This kind of depression, which should not be confused with clinical depression, is brought about by many factors, not the least of which is the idea that "I can never get what I want. I have no hope." Something always keeps you from achieving your goal, reaching your destination, knowing success.

We have learned our helplessness through our hopelessness. We are much like the adult circus elephant, several thousand pounds heavy and very strong, that is successfully tethered to a small stake by a comparatively small rope. From birth, the elephant has been trained to the tether. At first, a substantial chain attached to an equally substantial stake, taught the baby that no amount of tugging and pulling would break the chain. Every day, the lesson was the same. At some point in the elephant's training, the trainer began using a much smaller rope attached to a much smaller stake. It didn't matter. The elephant had long ago discovered how hopeless it was to pull against the restraint, so it no longer tried. What situations in your life have been like that? What lessons from your childhood continue to be huge chains that prevent you from breaking away? Have you noticed that the restraint no longer exists in reality?

Depression lives in the future, not in the present. If depression lived in the present, we would call it frustration or annoyance. If you keep your thinking in the here and the now, you will stand a much better chance of keeping depression out of your life. Evaluate your situation to see whether what limited you in the past limits you today.

Another feeling that frequently blocks us is envy. Simply stated, envy is wanting what someone else has, plus the belief that I can't have it. The best way to overcome this feeling is to work through the Steps. Read through the text in Step Seven, in which I talked about thinking and behaving as though you are successful, much like we "dress for success." More than one hundred years ago, William James, the psychologist, said that it was possible to control our feelings by controlling our actions. The elephant could not act in proportion to its confinement. It could not understand that it could be free with very little energy. You can understand that and behave as though the bonds of alcoholism are shredding, day by day.

You don't always know what you're feeling in sobriety, and you can't always control your feelings, but you can control what you do. The Japanese form of therapy, Morita, says there are only three things that are key to therapy and to life: 1) feel your feelings, 2) know your purpose, and 3) do what needs to be done. If you practice the introspection technique and the action technique, and share with your sponsor and in meetings, you will see results in the area of your feelings that will amaze you.

9
Sponsors, Buddies, and Other Techniques

The first few years of my recovery were so crazy, so difficult. I am convinced that I would not be here today had it not been for my sponsors and buddies. There were many sponsors, among them an alcoholism counselor and a telephone lineman. But the sponsor who was with me for seven years, through the very worst of my early recovery, was Carl. He looked like a combination of Albert Einstein and Mark Twain. He wasn't perfect, but he was always there for me. Carl was gentle and very understanding. I felt comfortable telling him anything. Carl also was the person most responsible for saving my life, and I shall be forever grateful to him.

For a time, I was on the psychiatric ward of the local mental-health center. In the days of my early recovery, the generally accepted treatment for alcoholics was to prescribe pills. Among others, I had Valium to keep me calm and sleeping pills to help me through nights of fitful sleep. I was so addicted to the pills that I carried a bottle of them in my pocket, always at the ready. I was on so many prescription

drugs I couldn't imagine myself drug free if my life de-
pended on it. My life did depend on being drug free. Carl
understood this, even though he didn't do drugs. He told
me, quite simply, to turn my life and my will over to the
care of God, and amazing things could happen. "But," he
said, "I forgot. You don't believe in those things, do you"
In fact, I didn't. I felt that God had abandoned me.

One night I thought about killing myself. The possibility was very real for me. I looked out my window. It was
January, and I was in New Jersey. Snow had covered us
over for weeks, which was reason enough to despair. As I
thought about hanging myself (a pipe behind the ceiling
tiles would have facilitated the job) I looked out my window. I saw green grass, not just snow. It was another moment of synchronicity. A sign of hope when I needed it
most. I had felt trapped. I didn't like where I was, and I
didn't trust myself not to get drunk on the outside. In my
drug-induced despair and desperation, I had a lucid thought:
I would have to listen, at least a little bit, to what people in
sobriety have been telling me about recovery. This acknow-
ledgment was my first true surrender.

When I was getting off the prescription drugs, mostly
tranquilizers, Carl would let me sleep over at his house because I had freaked out at my apartment. Today we call
what I had experienced an anxiety state, or panic disorder.
We didn't know much about those conditions then. I had
experienced a panic response to a situation that had been
traumatic; I had had a nightmare, awakened in a panic, and
felt like drinking. Carl saw me through many more occa-
sions of panic in the days to come, but he had been right.
With my surrender, some amazing things began to happen.
Meeting Dr. Claire Weeks, author of *Hope and Help for*

Your Nerves and *Peace from Nervous Suffering.* She coached me through a remarkable set of coincidences. Once I had "let go and let God," my life began to turn away from alcohol and drugs toward "clean" living.

Finding the Sponsor for You

Part of your steady recovery is knowing and accepting that you cannot travel the road to sobriety completely on your own. You must, of course, accept responsibility for your disease and for regaining your good health, but accepting help from others is essential. Sponsors can be an important part of your recovery, but you must select a sponsor carefully.

You could think of your sponsor as a mentor, although I think the word has become trite. The role of the sponsor reaches far beyond the mentor/teacher definition, from my point of view. The road to sobriety is scary, tough, and full of wrong turns and dead ends. My sponsor's role in my life has been as a spiritual guide, teacher, friend, and a father and brother figure. In whatever way I thought about the person, two things were true: my sponsor helped me to remain calm on my journey, and he never gave up on me when I took some of those wrong turns or headed toward a dead end. I have had many sponsors during my journey to sobriety, and the lessons, the strength from their support, their encouragement and wisdom live deep in my heart and mind. I owe the success in my life and this book to their constancy.

You should choose your sponsor carefully. Some of the best advice about sponsor selection comes from AA, which has more successful experience in the field than any program. AA says, for instance, that you should pick a

sponsor who has been sober for at least two years because
this length of time demonstrates some maturity in the individual. In my opinion, it takes this long for most people to
gain enough experience to talk you out of whatever problem you are having, such as wanting to drink, not talk you
into the drinking. Without some maturity and some determination to remain sober, the sponsor could have a detrimental effect on your recovery.

Your sponsor should be someone you can talk to
freely, someone you respect and someone you believe you
can trust. All three qualities are essential, because as you
express your thoughts and exchange ideas with your sponsor, you won't always agree. I didn't always agree with
Carl, but I respected him and trusted him enough to listen to
him. Early in my recovery, Carl told me that I was being
phony. I was cursing a lot at the time, and he told me that
the language was not part of me, that it was an act. Of
course, I got angry and ranted and cursed even more, but I
trusted him and respected him, so I calmed down, and we
talked.

You can get a handle on who might be a good sponsor
by listening to what people say in meetings. When you hear
someone whose ideas you respect and admire, approach
him or her and ask if he or she would sponsor you. If the
potential sponsor declines, don't take the answer as rejection of you as a person. Sponsors are people in their own
right, too. Your potential sponsor might be experiencing
constraints of his or her own or sponsoring several people
and believe that he or she could not be as helpful to and
supportive of you as you need. This has nothing to do with
you and everything to do with what's going on in the spon-

sor's life. More times than not, however, the potential sponsor will accept.

Clancy, a sponsor, tells a story about bringing the person he was sponsoring to meetings. At one speakers' meeting, they heard an Archie Bunker-type person hollering about not drinking. "Just put the plug in the jug! Don't drink! That is all! Just don't drink!" The speaker offered no advice beyond the declarations, repeated in various forms. On the way home, the person Clancy was sponsoring said, "I'm a little confused. You say I have to work the steps, and he says I don't. You are sober one year; he has been sober twenty years. Who is right?" Clancy just got quiet. He deposited the person at his home and drove away without answering the question. A similar thing happened at the next meeting: different speaker, same message. This time, Clancy, who had given the question considerable thought, was ready. He had matured a little in his thought and gained some insight in his own recovery. Clancy realized that both he and the speaker were right, but there was a significant difference in the attitudes and the resolve of the individuals. He told the person he was sponsoring, "You're right. You can go about it the way the speaker says. If you want to feel as miserable as he feels, don't work the steps. As for myself, I came in here feeling that miserable. I don't need any help feeling that bad. So, if you want to feel like him, don't work the steps."

This is the kind of feedback you need from a sponsor. You need to have him or her tell you what is good for you. The message might not, however, match what you want to hear. Look for a sponsor who can be honest, a person who won't sugar-coat the truth so that you are able to find an excuse not to do what you know is right and necessary to your recovery. This is one place to heed the adage "Never judge a book by its cover." Listen to what potential sponsors are saying to others as you visit meetings. Forget what they look like. The words from the sponsor, the reinforcement for what you do right, the encouragement to continue and to work the steps, the strength you gain from the sponsor are the important elements of the relationship.

One other point: Your sponsor does not have to be someone who attends your home meeting. He or she can be based in another meeting. Just look for the person who meets your needs and is qualified through at least two years of experience in a 12-step program.

Meetings with Your Sponsor

Try to meet with your sponsor at least once a week. Go out to dinner before the meeting. Get some "dashboard therapy" by talking in the car before the meeting. Have coffee together after the meeting. If you use these meetings with your sponsor effectively, they can help to change the course of your life.

Regardless of how often you meet with your sponsor keep these two things in mind. One, don't hold back. Talk honestly and openly about the things that are bothering you. If you withhold information, you give your sponsor a distorted picture of what's happening. Two, listen to everything your sponsor has to say. Don't tune out part of it because it isn't what you want to hear. Your sponsor, if he or she is a good one, will tell you what you need to hear, not just what you want to hear, to keep your life moving toward continued sobriety.

One other point about sponsors is this. If you and your sponsor stop hitting it off well, try to work through your difficulties, don't just "fire" your sponsor. As I said in a previous chapter, you must be selfish about your recovery, but you need to exercise some judgment. There is no point in getting rid of a sponsor because of a minor disagreement, although that does seem to be the rage these days. Your job is to get well, and the sponsor you selected might still be the right one to help you. You must keep your goal — sobriety — foremost in your mind.

Using the Buddy System

Sharing with your sponsor is one of the most effective methods I have found for rapid improvement in sober thinking. What do you do, though, if you cannot reach your sponsor? Sponsors have lives, too, and you might not get in touch with yours as quickly as you would like in a specific circumstance. One method I have used with great success is the buddy system. To use this technique, you find someone in AA, for instance, who is not your sponsor. Your buddy does not have to have as much sobriety as your sponsor because his or her role in your life is different. Six months sobriety is acceptable. The basic requirement for the buddy is that he or she attends 40,000 meetings a week. That is, of course, an exaggeration, but the implication is serious commitment to being sober. Your buddy should attend several meetings a week, have a sponsor, have a home group, and work the steps as much as possible. I have achieved more success from using the buddy system than almost any other method, with the exception of working with Carl.

Mitch was my buddy. He meant a lot to me and to my life. He was sixty-something and about 120, soaking wet.

Once upon a time he had been a diamond cutter, but now he worked as a bartender in a bucket-of-blood-type tavern. He did everything that my sponsor did and more. He kept me from leaving my mail-room job when I got fed up with it and was so discouraged that I wasn't sure whether I could go on. Mitch wasn't feeling well when I went to see him. He suffered from emphysema and continued to smoke. But he gave me some time that day and forcefully delivered some important advice. He told me to quit running from my problems and to face them down. I tried to use my "intellect" to turn his thoughts around to my way of thinking. He got mad or exasperated or something, and he hollered at me to "let it happen, you flacky bastard!" The circumstances, mine and his, made his words among the most important in my life.

In his book *I Ain't Well, But I Sure Am Better,* my friend and mentor, Jess Lair, recommends enlisting five friends as buddies. The number can be from four to six, but it is best to have more than two. Of course, this is a matter of practicality. If one buddy doesn't work out in a particular situation or the situation requires extra help, you still have others to call upon. You also don't want to burn out your buddy. Let's say, for instance, that you broke up with your girlfriend (boyfriend), or you lost your job, or your job has become miserably difficult, at best. Let's say, too, that you are going to meetings every night to give yourself some balance. If you talked to one buddy on Monday, you could talk to a different buddy on Tuesday, and yet another buddy on Wednesday. By the time you get back in touch with the first buddy, he or she will be fresh to listen and to help. Too often, people in recovery, either in or out of a program, have only one or two buddies they can rely on. As a result of this exclusivity, they end up wearing out their buddies.

I cannot emphasize enough the importance and the effectiveness of both the sponsor and the buddy system. Both provide continual example of the cliché "You are helped by the people you help." For a year, I took Bill, the guy this book is dedicated to, to meetings. He helped me to focus. Hopefully, I helped him, too. This is the way the program goes. Today you will help someone who is helping you; another day, when you are a sponsor or a buddy, you still will be helping someone who is helping you.

Other Valuable Techniques

Be a Friend

To learn what sobriety is like, teach it to someone else. In early recovery, one good way to work your 12-step program and to learn how to develop these steps is to take someone around to meetings. Do this not as a sponsor but as a friend. I have taken many persons in early sobriety to meetings. My time with them helped me to keep my focus, to learn a little more, and to strengthen my recovery.

Fellowship and Internal Techniques

Fellowship is a powerful component of your recovery. It is fostered by attending meetings, week after week, and getting to know the people in the meeting. Getting to know people is an art, and it certainly is not always easy to do. It is, nonetheless, easier if you keep some simple thoughts in mind about the dynamics of people in groups. As Clancy, the sponsor, says, people generally look around the room to assess the crowd. Even the most timid of souls will take a furtive peek at the collection of people in the room. Who appears to be confident, or shy, or standoffish? Who is in charge? Who appears to be in charge? Who is as wounded as you are? You will have your own method of assessing the individuals.

If your disease is like mine, and I know that it is, you will end up comparing your insides with someone else's outsides. Your tender, innermost feelings run right smack into the defense mechanisms that some of those people have carefully cultivated for a decade or two, or more. In reality, you aren't going to meet someone who looks as sensitive as you feel. This difference would be almost comical, except for the fact that it drives people who need each other farther apart.

The way to develop fellowship is to *identify,* not to compare. When we are in trouble, we tend to compare. Clancy says the best test of how you are doing is to note how the people at a meeting appear to you. If they seem to behave like fools, then, more than likely, the fool is you because you aren't sober. If, on the other hand, everyone seems to be all right, then you probably are sober.

Fellowship and External Techniques

When you first enter the room, say "hello" to as many people as you can. However, because people are in various stages of recovery and have greater stages of the disease than others, be careful whom you talk with. Until you are sober for a while, stick to your own gender. The reason for this is, that the addictive person, which you are, can easily exchange addictions and develop a codependency in which you substitute addictions. This means that if, early in your recovery, you center on a member of the opposite sex, you probably will end up engaged in romantic and sexual encounters, rather than in fellowship in the sense that it is intended here. Of course, many in recovery ignore this rule and set their recovery back while they pursue this side issue. A year is a good length of time to wait before you extend your lines of fellowship. During that year, you will have kept your recovery on track.

Specific Techniques: Being Friendly

The more you identify with others, not compare with others, the closer you will feel to them, and the more you will feel the sense of belonging. For instance, after a meeting spend some time talking with people. Extend your hand in friendship and greeting and introduce yourself. In the beginning, it might be hard to do and some of your buttons might get pushed. You might, for instance, feel frightened or insecure. There is, however, no way through this stage, except to do it.

When I was at the lowest point in my life, as a result of my drinking, I went to a meeting. I saw this guy in the parking lot. I motioned toward the building and asked him if God was in those rooms. I guess I did it because I really needed a Higher Power. I was so burned out and fragile, that if this guy had laughed at me, I probably would not have gone to the meeting. He didn't laugh. Instead, his reply was gentle and friendly. "Yes, those of us that go here believe that God is inside these rooms." That gesture of friendliness made the difference to me at that moment. Your gesture of friendship could be just as powerful and important.

Shared Focus: How to Start a Conversation

How do you eat an elephant? You eat an elephant one hairy, gray bite at a time. You've surely heard that quip at least once in your lifetime. This same philosophy could apply to developing a friendship. A friendship doesn't happen in an instant. It develops through one conversation at a time. As you spend time at meetings, you will get to know more and more of the people there. You might identify with something that a participant said and begin a conversation about that topic.

Typical conversation starters, as psychologists tell us, include a shared focus, or whatever is in front of both of you. For example, you might comment on the meeting right after it's over: "I really liked what the speaker had to say about his recovery." That opens the door to conversation. Follow that with a statement about what you especially liked, such as his words about his sponsor, or what helped him to let go and let God, something specific. Remember, that the person to whom you are speaking might be as timid as you, and the response to your first statement might be nothing more than, "Yeah, me, too." Your recovery is in your hands, and you must make every effort to keep your recovery moving ahead. Taking the initiative in conversations is a good way to do that.

Another technique to use in starting a conversation is self-disclosure. In his book *In and Out of the Garbage Pail,* Frederick Perls, originator of Gestalt Therapy, said that he could find out anything about anybody in 15 minutes. All he had to do was to talk about himself. So, disclose something about yourself. Your prospective friend might reply, "Me, too. I thought I could have a drink once in a while." And the conversation begins, much like a game of catch.

Too often, people will try to open a conversation with a monologue, or they ask questions, and the other person begins to feel like he or she is being interrogated. By using self-disclosure, especially disclosure about how you felt early in your recovery, how the meetings made you feel, or how you feel now about meetings and your participation in the 12-step program, you start an exchange of information.

Come Early, Stay Late

In you come to meetings at least 15 minutes early and leave a minimum of 15 minutes after the meeting is over, you will see results in direct proportion to your efforts. You should do this in the beginning of your recovery, no matter what meeting you attend. Later on, you can drop the 15 minutes before the meeting and just keep to the after-meeting stay. This open-ended time allows you to meet new people and to discuss whatever is on your mind. Start small and build up. Suppose you really are interested in talking to someone with good sobriety, but you feel too intimidated. What do you do? Start talking with someone who is not quite so threatening and work your way up. This technique works when you are looking for someone to talk to or someone to be your sponsor. Say you are comfortable talking to your buddy, so you do that. Then you talk with someone who has been sober a little longer. By taking these smaller steps and being comfortable with them, you will achieve greater growth than if you try to make the leap to someone who has been sober for many years. You should not, however, shy away from talking to the veteran of sobriety. If you can do it, do it. As always, your objective is your recovery, and you must be selfish enough and determined enough about your recovery to take giant steps along with the small ones.

Telephone Therapy

What do you do if you cannot make it to a meeting? Try telephone therapy. Engage someone in a telephone conversation about your recovery issues. Suppose you are really uptight and need to share. Call your sponsor. Call your buddy. Call one of your AA contacts or a 12-step contact that you met through a conversation at a meeting. Use the same techniques that you used when you started a conversation at a meeting.

A word of caution: Do not use telephone therapy as a continued replacement for attending meetings. Although some talking on the phone is better than no talking, the human contact is important in your early recovery. You need to develop the skills to be with people in a positive way, and that can be done only by meeting people face to face.

10
Stress Reduction

Let's take a journey to the time, some 50,000 years ago, when our ancestors roamed Northern Africa. Uncle Nikanam sets out to hunt the family's dinner. He isn't thrilled about hunting a saber-toothed tiger, but the family needs food. Uncle Nikanam, accompanied by a huge dose of stress, leaves the cave for the hunt. Several things happen to Uncle Nikanam as he tracks dinner. His blood pressure goes up, and his breathing become very rapid. His muscles tense, his heart beats rapidly, and he begins to sweat. The stress, which begins to show itself in anger and fear, becomes so consuming that his digestion slows. If the fear becomes acute enough, Uncle Nikanam might lose control of his bladder and bowels.

Some good things, too, would be happening to Uncle Nikanam during this period of stress. Special infection-fighting hormones would be released so that his chances of surviving an infection would increase if he were injured in battle. The blood would drain from his hands and feet to reduce the pain he would feel, should he be attacked and an extremity severed, to reduce the flow of blood from his body. His body and his senses would wind up like a spring.

His vision would become very focused, very narrow, and very concentrated. Colors would appear more vivid. He would be more sensitive to loud noises and keyed to react. All of this would happen to help Uncle Nikanam carry out his decision to kill or be killed — the fight-or-flight response to stress. Then, when he has killed dinner, dragged it home and eaten, the effect of the stress would result in Uncle Nikanam sleeping for 20 or 30 hours to allow his body to regain its balance.

Today, few of us face such essential, life-threatening stress, but we choose to induce it or to enhance it by taking drugs or alcohol. Cocaine or speed revs the fight-or-flight response. Depressants, such as alcohol or heroin, slow it down. Heroin can, in fact, slow the bodily functions to such a degree that death results. Alcohol can do the same thing, but it takes different conditions and is much more difficult to accomplish.

A big difference exists between what Uncle Nikanam experienced and what we put ourselves through. The fight-or-flight response was a normal occurrence in the life of Uncle Nikanam and his friends, and it had some normal limits that rarely were exceeded and some normal consequences. Life was simple, and he followed nature's course. Now, we tinker with the laws of physics.

Remember your science teacher telling you that "for every action, there is an equal and opposite reaction"? Well, that's what we tinker with in our alcoholism or our drug addiction. Take your nervous system, for instance. The nervous system is like a spring. When you tense and work under stress, the spring pulls back. You're too stressed, you tell yourself. You drink some alcohol. The spring returns to normal and then relaxes a little too much.

Now you experience stress because of the alcohol, and you are on the physics roller coaster. When you take a stimulant, such as cocaine, the opposite is true. The stimulant tricks your body into thinking that a modern-day saber-toothed tiger is in front of you, and the effect of the drug activates the fight-or-flight response. Once the "danger" is over, your body craves rest. You become depressed, or even suicidal. You are on a different physics roller coaster, but the results are the same. The fight-or-flight response has been triggered.

The trouble is, even though we tinker with this response chemically, the response is an inborn part of you. As far as your body is concerned, you still are roaming the windswept plains of Northern Africa, club in hand, before modern civilization began. That sort of puts you in a bind. If your boss tells you to work faster and produce more, for example, your heart rate increases, your palms sweat, your digestion ceases, your muscles tense. You are ready to fight or flee. The spring is wound. Your saber-toothed tiger could be just around the corner. If the tiger turns out to be your boss, you can't grab up your briefcase, clobber your boss on the head, take him home as a trophy, and then sleep for 20 or 30 hours. You have to find an acceptable way to deal with your tiger, your stress.

Looking at Stress/Fear

One of the best explanations of stress I have found comes from Hayns Selye in *Stress and Distress*. He defines stress as the body's response to any demand, either positive or negative, placed upon it. (Notice that he says "body," not "mind.") Getting fired can be stressful, so can a promotion. Getting married can be stressful, so can getting a divorce. In its best form, stress can strengthen you. What takes its toll on you is the "distress," says Selye. The difference is this: Stress is tension plus relaxation, with the resolution of the conflict that created the stress. Distress is tension with no resolution of the conflict and no periods of relaxation. Stress without resolution of the conflict and no relaxation results in distress.

People in early recovery (detoxification or the first AA or other group meeting) often see saber-toothed tigers, huge stress creators, where none exist. For more than six years during my addiction, my saber-toothed tiger was panic. I was unable to attend to do many things because my tiger was so stressful. Before I found a way to deal with my stress, I was unemployed and unemployable. A series of events put me in contact with Dr. Claire Weeks, author of *Hope and Help for Your Nerves* and of *Peace from Nervous Suffering*. At first, I only read her books. Later we talked on the telephone and corresponded. She wound up saving my life. Dr. Weeks says that three things contribute to nervous illness, which grips us all at one time or another. The first is stress, which we have touched upon. The second is bewilderment, wondering "Why is this happening to me?" The third thing is fear, or, rather, the fear of feeling fear.

Fear is a powerful emotion that entangles us in a destructive cycle. According to Dr. Weeks, when we experience the first fear, an instant later, we also experience a second fear. For example, you have been sensitized over the years to fear a sight, a sound, a smell, a memory, a word, or a tone of voice. The fear produces a rush of adrenalin, a chemical that, in itself, produces fear. The second fear results in words like "Oh, no! Oh, no! Here it comes again!" or "What if (happens) and I flip out?" The adrenalin is pumping, and you are rolling along on a cycle of fear that powers itself.

When you stop the second fear, the "Oh, no! Not again!" you stop feeding the first fear, according to Dr. Weeks, and the first fear will eventually die a natural death. When you deprive your body of the adrenalin rush that feeds the fear, all fear can do is to die.

Another method is to relax when the fear reaches its greatest pressure. Dr. Weeks emphasizes that it is essential that you not fight the fear. Relaxing will stop the flow of adrenalin; fighting the fear keeps the adrenalin flowing.

How do you stop the second fear? By recognizing what is happening. It will take some time and some serious attention to your reactions, but you can overcome the fear of fear. Dr. Weeks offers a four-part, powerful method to help you to recover from anxiety, which you can incorporate into a 12-step program. The method has four key phrases: face, accept, float, let time pass.

1. Face your fears, without becoming afraid of what you feel.

2. Accept your fears. Resign yourself to your fears, surrender to them. Accepting your fears has a calming effect upon the nervous system and, practiced over a period of time, will work in your recovery. This technique is, of course, like Step One. You accept that you are powerless over your alcoholism and your life becomes unmanageable as a result of your drinking; you accept that your fears are going to surface, but the "Oh, no! Not again!" doesn't have to follow.

3. Float with your fears. This technique relates to the third step in a 12-step program. When a disturbing thought intrudes, picture yourself floating on a raft in warm water on a pleasantly warm day. Let the troublesome thought float beside you on the raft. Don't tune in to it; don't try to tune it out. Just let it lay there, with no value at all. The less often you give value to your fears, the less often you will climb aboard the cycle of fear, adrenalin, fear, adrenalin, and on and on. If you float your fears long enough, you will be less anxiety ridden. I used this technique to bring me out of a state of chronic anxiety. Instead of allowing my fear of meetings to start the cycle rolling, I would float into a meeting and float out of it.

4. Let time pass. There are many ways to say this. Dr. Weeks says that we should not be impatient with time. In AA, they say "Give time time." And surely you have heard "This too shall pass." This technique truly is a case of letting go and letting God. If you diligently employ the techniques mentioned in this book and give time time, you will put your "Stress/Fear Cycle" into the closet in your mind, because it no longer has value to you.

Other Fear/Stress-Reduction Techniques

Two other ways to confront fear are flooding and systematic desensitization. Flooding is like jumping into the water and letting it flood over you until you surface. You face your fears all at once, and let them wash over you until you rise above them. Systematic desensitization is like putting your toe in the water, then your foot, then your leg and so on. You face your fears gradually. Both techniques are effective. I suggest that you use whatever is appropriate to the circumstances and your needs at the time.

When I was in early recovery, going to meetings made me feel like I was cracking up. My anxiety level was so high it would rate a 10 (one is the least) on the anxiety scale. It was the most afraid I had ever been in my life. There was no way for me to go at this fear one piece at a time. I had to tackle it all at once. So I flooded into the meeting. In my mind, I flooded up the stairs and into the room all at once, not gradually.

I used systematic desensitization to overcome my fear of being in a store. I would go into a store and wait for my anxiety level to rise. When the anxiety became too much, I would leave the store. Because constant exposure to the thing that you fear lessens the fear, systematic desensitization might be the tool for you to use.

It is important for you to remember that these techniques will work, regardless of what level of fear you are experiencing.

Fear Associated with Social Phobia

I experienced phobias, or exaggerated fear responses to a situation. Most phobias have some element of real fear attached to them, such as the fear of spiders, or the fear of elevators. The spider could bite you, and the elevator could fall. We also experience social phobias. Someone who has a phobia of crowds might say, "I am not afraid of crowds. I just don't like them." The person is not comfortable being in a crowd and usually will avoid the experience.

Let's say you have trouble going to meetings. For the ease of explanation, let's make them AA meetings because these meetings are pretty uniform in format and in expectations across the country. You might try both flooding and systematic desensitization. First, make a list of things you fear at meetings. Rate your fears from one to however many fears you have written, with one being the greatest fear. For the sake of discussion, say that you fear going into the meetings. Start by standing at the back of the room until you feel comfortable there. You might do this for several meetings. (Remember to give time time.) When you are comfortable with being in the room, go get a cup of coffee. You will have had a chance to see how the system works at the coffee pot, so you should feel more comfortable with that exercise. Next time, sit a little closer to the front of the room. Even a row or two closer is an improvement. Approach each of your ranked fears in a similar fashion. If you confront your fears in stages, you'll be more successful in facing the most difficult fears later on.

Reducing Stress Through Transcendental Meditation

Another effective stress-reduction technique is transcendental meditation, or TM. This technique gained popularity in the early '60s through the famous guru Maharishi. Many famous people, from the Beatles to Clint Eastwood, have practiced TM. This technique is useful because the biochemistry of the alcoholic in early recovery is out of balance, and mood swings occur. Our addiction has rendered useless our normal coping mechanisms. Relaxation without alcohol is difficult for us. Anything we can do to calm our system will help to improve the chemical balance and return our coping skills. Deep relaxation, which is the basis of TM, practiced consistently over a period of time, will have a tremendous positive effect.

Dr. Herbert Benson in *The Relaxation Response,* says meditation has three basic elements: the mantra (the word you repeat), the thought and the mantra, and just thought. You arrive at each stage in its own time, and practice makes the difference in your success. Benson recommends having a passive mind set to start the process. This is one time when being assertive will get in your way.

How do you start TM, when do you do it, and how much do you do it? Begin by seating yourself in comfortable surroundings, a place where you will have a minimum of 20 minutes quiet time. This is the length of time recommended for those who are new to the technique. Select a word, such as "one," or "light," any word that has no emotional attachment for you. Close your eyes and repeat the mantra. Do not block thoughts; do not try to bring in thoughts. Just repeat the mantra. If you are saying the mantra and thinking thoughts, this is okay. When you realize that you have stopped saying the mantra, simply go back to it. As you become skilled in TM, you will experience calm throughout your body.

A note of caution: TM is a part of your recovery regimen. It complements the speaker meetings, the steps,

H.A.L.T., the fellowship, all of whatever program you have adopted.

Time Management to Reduce Stress (One Task at a Time)

It is common for alcoholics in early recovery to have difficulty managing their time effectively. I had trouble with time management, and I have helped many to stop having trouble with it. Basically, time managed poorly results in too little time to accomplish all that needs to be done, which results in stress. You can manage your time, even though you might think now that you have too many demands, too many spontaneous events, too much of everything.

Begin by making a to-do list. This list alone will help to improve your effective use of time by 25 percent the first time you use it. Write down the single most important thing you have to do today. Then ask yourself, "If I could do only two things, what would the next thing be?" Continue this process until you have six or seven items. Take a look at the list and decide if you really have the list ranked as you want it. If not, renumber the items. This will help you to give priority to your activities and to understand which things should come first. Brian Tracy, a prominent seminar leader, suggests you ask yourself this question, as you make your list: If I were called out of town for one week and could do only one (two, three, etc.) thing(s) before I leave, what would it be?

To help you start your to-do list, here is an example:

- 1. Write fourth step
- 2. Clean out car (apartment, etc.)

- 3. Go to 12-step meeting (noon)
- 4. Look for work
- 5. Go to night 12-step meeting
- 6. Read something for fun (enlightenment, etc.)

Start with your number one. Do the task completely. Do not move on to the second item until the first one is finished, even if you must stay on that task all day. Your progress will be more consistent and stronger if you maintain focus and don't skip from one item to another.

In the sample list, I have included two meetings. Whether you attend AA meetings or some other group meeting, the alcoholic in early recovery generally needs more than one meeting to help keep the stress in check.

After you have made your to-do list and have set about the tasks, ask yourself if you are accomplishing as much as you would like. In most cases, you won't be, because you have slipped off track. Too many things on the list are going undone. When this happens, and it will, ask yourself whether what you are doing is the best use of your time. If you are watching television instead of looking for a job, for instance, you have slipped off the track. Is watching television the best use of your time? Sure, you can crack wise about the value of television, but the truth is, your time in front of the television won't help you to find a job and it won't help to pay your bills. You must be as honest with yourself at this time as you were when you accepted your alcoholism.

Another method to get you back on track comes from the billionaire W. Clement Stone, who attributes much of his success to the affirmation "Do it now! Do it now!" If you say the words and do the deed, you will be back on track.

Using the 80/20 Rule to Reduce Stress

The second time-management technique to consider is the 80/20 Rule, also known as Perado's Principle. Alfred Perado, a nineteenth-century economist, discovered that any system of activity, whether the activity is government, business, or personal, 20 percent of certain efforts will result in 80 percent of the results. Conversely, he said, 80 percent of certain efforts will result in 20 percent of the results. So, to manage your time effectively, you should focus on the 20 percent that will reap the 80 percent return on your investment of time.

As an example of how the 80/20 rule works, perhaps the only thing you did right or well for the day was to attend a 12-step meeting. In the overall scheme of things, it represents a small amount of time. Nevertheless, the time you invested might have put you on the right track in managing your fear, or meeting some phobia head on. Talking with your sponsor is another activity that requires a small amount of time, but the results of the investment could be substantial. Many times my conversation with Carl, talking about the things that were a problem for me, was the only thing I did right that day.

Reducing Stress through Forced Efficiency

I often meet people in recovery who are trying to catch up on their life by adding activities without subtracting any. In fact, I was one of those people. I was studying Aikido, a form of martial art, in addition to working full-time, maintaining an active part-time seminar business, a part-time private practice, and going to graduate school. Talk about stress! I realized that I had to drop something from my schedule. The decision was a difficult one for me. I dropped Aikido, which I loved, in order to put more time into my studies, which would be over soon. Then I could devote more time to my professional life. I also took a little time for myself, which reduced my stress still more.

Reducing Stress with Swiss Cheese

There you sit, a major project in front of you, and you are unable to begin. The help-wanted sections from the major newspapers in your area lay untouched on the kitchen table. You have put off this project because finding a job seems an overwhelming task. I've got news for you. It will continue to be an overwhelming task until you begin to punch holes in it. Start small. Spend five or 10 minutes with one help-wanted section. Reward yourself with a walk or a little television watching, then spend another five to 10 minutes with the help-wanted section. Chances are, once you begin the task, you probably will spend longer than five or 10 minutes on it and reduce your load (and your stress) by a third or a half. The person who encouraged me to write this book suggested that I write two pages a day, when I said that writing an entire book was too scary a prospect. Two pages a day didn't seem like a lot. Two by two, the pages were written. As we say in recovery, life is hard by the yard, but it is a cinch by the inch.

Reducing Stress through Goal Setting

People in my seminars repeatedly ask me how can they possibly set goals if they are to live one day at a time.

You do that one day at a time, too. For the past 10 years, I have been working out. I have goals that pertain to my weight-lifting activity. When I first started to visit the weight room, I was so intimidated I would go to the room reluctantly. I felt totally out of place. But, I persisted, one day at a time. I still live each day, but I am looking forward to my future in working out. I have a new hobby that gives me much satisfaction and goals toward which I can work.

Alan Larken, in his book *How to Get Effective Control of Your Time and Your Life,* suggests this way to set goals. You will need some sheets of paper and about 15 to 20 minutes. On the top of one sheet write "My Five-Year Goals." Give yourself exactly five minutes to write everything that you would like to do, be, or have in the next five years. Put everything on the list, from the most ridiculous to the most serious. Some examples might be: obtain a college degree, sail the seven seas, build houses, write a book, learn to fly. Don't edit your list; just write as quickly as the ideas come into your head.

Take the second sheet of paper and write "My One-Year Goals" at the top. Give yourself five minutes and write all that you would like to do, be or have in the next year. Do not edit your thoughts; just write them as quickly as they come.

On the third sheet of paper, write "My Six-Month Goals" at the top. Before you write these goals, ask yourself this question: If I knew that I was in perfect health and that I would be struck dead by lightning in six months, what would be my goals in those six months? Set your timer for five minutes and write those goals. Don't edit, just write.

Now, go back to your list of five-year goals and circle the three that are most important to you. Do the same with your one-year and six-month goals. This exercise is structured so that you have the opportunity to get in touch with what you feel deeply about and value the most. (The six-month goals, by the way, will reflect the values most important to you.) Some of the men in the rehabilitation unit where I work say they would get drunk if they had only six months to live. Others say they would stay sober, and then they tell how they would spend those sober days. What is most important for you to know and to focus on is, these are your lists, your values.

On a fresh piece of paper, write the nine goals that you have circled. So, now what? There's an old saying. "Obstacles are what you see when you take your mind off the goal." The best way to keep your mind on your goals is to set some action plans for them. Let's say one of your goals is to be sober for one year, one day at a time. How are you going to accomplish that goal? What actions will get you there? The list of actions doesn't have to be detailed; it just needs actions. You plan to stay sober for one year, one day at a time by (1) getting a sponsor, (2) getting a home group, (3) by regularly going to meetings, (4) by working the steps, and (5) by getting a buddy. If you walk the path toward sobriety by the methods of this plan, you will succeed.

When you set a goal, put the goal in mind, but don't try too hard, because trying too hard will mess up the process of developing your instincts. In Aikido, we learn to use our opponent's strength against him, in order to subdue him. When you try too hard to win, you lose your effectiveness. The same is true of goals. Don't be too concerned about the outcome.

If you wonder how accurate is this method of determining which things have the greatest value, I can tell you, with confidence, that if you were to take a three-day seminar in goal-setting, the results would be very similar to those you obtained with this exercise.

Goal Setting by the Short Form

Brian Tracy, the seminar leader, taught me this way to quickly set goals. The method takes about five minutes a day. First, when you get up in the morning or just before you go to bed, write down your goals for the day. If you do this before bed, you are, of course, writing the goals for the next day. Keep the list to five items. Second, reread your list at the end of the day. Third, ask yourself what you did that day to move yourself closer to your goals. And fourth, ask yourself what you would do differently if you could repeat the day.

This simple method will help you to achieve your goals faster than almost any other method, in proportion to the time you put into it.

You Are Responsible

When you set a goal, it is important that you commit to the goal. In *Reality Therapy,* William Glasser states that successful people give their words and make no excuses. Addicts, however, give their word plus reasonable excuses as to why they broke their word. You are responsible for your choice, your good health, the cure for your disease. Commit to your goal of sobriety.

Brian Tracy tells about a mental-programming technique that works to set old ways behind you. He says that to start our day, we need two things: a high-protein meal for our body and positive pictures for our mind. Begin your day with 15 to 30 minutes of spiritual, educational, or motivational reading, something that will help you to improve the quality of your sobriety. This is the technique I use to program my mind for productivity. Over time, this technique will help you change the very basis of how you view the world and will significantly reduce the amount of stress you experience.

11
Assertiveness

It has been said that we alcoholics are very good at being passive (not saying anything) and at being aggressive (blowing our tops), but we are not good at being assertive (expressing our feelings in a positive way). We talked briefly about assertiveness in Chapter Nine, but because this quality is a strategic one, I want to more fully explain it.

As I work with alcoholics in rehabilitation, one of the most common things they tell me is "I'm really easy going." What they really mean is that they are passive. They don't consider that they, or what they want, are important. In group sessions, these members will say that they are "just listening," which is a passive response to being in a group in which there is much interaction. To bring this explanation closer to your life, when someone causes you to be angry, for instance, and you don't respond, you are being passive. If someone says to you, "Oh, you wouldn't understand anyway. You're an alcoholic," and you don't tell that person that he or she has hurt your feelings, you are being passive. Or, if you don't express your needs in reference to what you want or need, you are being passive. Passivity demonstrates an attitude of "I'm not important; you are important."

On the other hand, if you blow your top over a situation that is relatively minor in relation to the harm you experienced, then you are being aggressive. Or if someone at work does something you don't like, and you lose your temper and shout at that person, you are being aggressive. This behavior says that "I'm important; you are not important."

The Assertiveness Model

The model of assertiveness shows that you count and you believe that the other person counts, too. In the examples above, you would tell the person that, yes, you might be an alcoholic, but you are capable of understanding many things, and you would prefer not to be spoken to in that way. Or you might tell the coworker that what he or she did to you was uncalled for, and that you do not appreciate being treated in that way. This model shows that both you and the other person count. In picture form, these three models look like this:

Passive	Assertive	Aggressive
I'm not important.	You're important.	You're not important.
You're important.	I'm important.	I'm important.

Why Is It Important to Be Assertive?

Because self-expression is vital to our sense of who we are, it is important that we express our own reality. Each of us has a unique point of view. Each of us is the product of our experiences, our environment, our genes. No two persons, even those in the same family, have exactly the same perspective of how life should be lived, what constitutes good or evil, or what is right or wrong. When we leave this life, our unique point of view will go with us. Your point of view and mine contribute to the overall experiences shared by those around us.

There is a direct relation between assertiveness — self-expression — and anger reduction and sobriety. Self-assertiveness, in the very best sense of the word, is you being able to express your point of view, not to change the other person, but to say how you see things. Each human being has the need to describe what he or she sees, experiences, feels, or thinks. The more you express yourself, the better you feel about yourself.

You Can Learn to Be Assertive

You could begin by digging into your past to learn why you are not assertive. Some alcohol counselors would take you down that road. I prefer to begin where you are now and build toward your future.

The basic tool for being assertive is "I" language. This means that when you talk with someone, you say, "I think . . . ," "I feel . . . ," "I know that . . . ," "It seems to me that . . ." Avoid, whenever possible, language like, "You should . . . ," "You ought to . . . ," comments that are "you" centered. The only person about whom you can speak with any authority is yourself. As I tell the people in rehab group sessions, "Talk about yourself, guys, not about someone else." Many of us have been taught that talking about oneself is wrong, that we should not put ourselves in front. As a result, speaking about ourselves, even our points of view, seems like foreign ground. For many, it is foreign territory, but, like learning a foreign language, it can become part of your life. It does take practice, however, just as learning any new skill takes practice. Like facing your fears or some displeasurable occurrence in your life, constant exposure to the thing you fear or find disgusting lessens your fear or your aversion.

Of all the lessons I have learned on my way to sobriety, the lesson in assertiveness was among the best and most effective. Learning to be assertive can start with something as basic as a conversation. In Chapter Nine, you learned about starting conversations. Reread that part of the chapter. Learning to be assertive and a good conversationalist sort of work hand in hand. The more assertive you become in sharing how you see things, without denying someone else the right to his or her viewpoint, the more skilled you will be in conversations.

How does this work? Let's say someone offends you. Reject the impulse to blow your top. Instead, begin by describing the event and telling the person how you feel about his or her behavior. For example, you might say, "When you didn't show up on time for our meeting, I felt angry. You made me think that you didn't respect me." Or you could be more direct and to the point. "Your being late really bothers me. Please don't do it again." If the person is your friend, he or she will probably make the change. If the person is not your friend, the tardiness probably will continue. People say and do hurtful things. If the person continues to do and say hurtful things to you, then you have a decision to make. As they say, actions speak louder than words. If the actions continue to be negative and abusive, maybe you need to re-evaluate your relationship with that person.

Using "I" language in conversations is one way to begin assertiveness in a small way. Another such experience would be to return an item to a store. Keep it simple. "I am returning this shirt because the sleeves are too short," or whatever. You don't have to say anything more than that. Just express yourself.

Confrontational Expression

Confrontation is not fun in any situation, but expressing yourself, being assertive, might mean that you have to confront the person who has verbally abused you. For instance, someone in a business meeting crudely remarks something like, "What is wrong with you, stupid?" or "If I was as dense as you are, I would quit my job and live in the woods!" These might be extremes in comments, but you might experience something of this sort. What do you do? Nothing at the moment if other people are present. Remain calm and either look straight ahead or look at him with an "I see you" expression. Don't respond to his remarks at that moment. Confrontation with others around usually makes things worse, because the person who made the crude remark becomes defensive. He's kind of like the bully on the playground. As long as he has an audience, he will continue his abuse with bravado. Confront him alone, and he is a different person, because he isn't playing to an audience. It's just you and him.

When you get this person alone, remain casual. Shrug your shoulders and say something like, "What's going on? This is the second time today that you have taken a pot shot at me." Look him directly in the eyes, maintain eye contact, and don't say another word. Two things are important here. First, the shrug of the shoulders, according to anthropologists, is a universal sign of nonverbal nonaggression in every major culture. Second, maintaining the eye contact and the silence is a long-used technique among those who must make the sale, or overcome an argument. The person who breaks the silence or the eye contact loses. Don't let the person bluff you with phrases like, "I don't know what you are talking about," or "You're too sensitive," or "Your imagining something." These are invitations to an argument that will go nowhere, and you want to stay on track. Maintain the eye contact and say, calmly and clearly, "You called me stupid in front of my peers, and the remark was both crude and unnecessary." Then walk away. Don't get drawn into the bully's argument.

Two other techniques you can use in confronting the person are the "broken record" and "fogging." The broken record technique is pretty much as the name implies. You repeat the phrase until you wear down the other person. For example, the boardroom bully says he doesn't know what you are talking about. You repeat your early comment. "Your remark upset me." Don't add any kind of explanation. Your viewpoint is all that you need to express. He might continue to badger you with his "innocence," but repeat the remark, then walk away. This technique is particularly effective with someone whom you consider to be a superior verbal opponent. Use this technique to avoid trapping yourself in repetitious phrases.

Fogging is a little different. With fogging, you admit to the possibility or the probability that something might be true. For instance, if the person repeats that you are too sensitive, you could reply, "Maybe I am sensitive, but your remark was still crude and unnecessary." You have admitted to your sensitivity and taken away a gimmick to draw you into an argument. You have fogged his thinking, and you have repeated your comment.

Both techniques allow you to assert yourself. If practiced each time you must state your viewpoint, both techniques will become a part of you. The welcome side effect of being assertive is that your self-esteem will increase.

Constructive and Destructive Criticism

Harold Bloomfield, in his book *The Achilles Syndrome,* writes that constructive criticism is meant to help someone; destructive criticism tears down the person's self-esteem. While you practice your assertiveness, please keep this thought in mind: The other person might consider what you say as criticism. How you say what you want to say makes a big difference. "I" language is the language of constructive criticism, and constructive criticism focuses on the specific event and is behavior specific. For example, "When you didn't take out the garbage (the event), I felt bad." You can add why it made you feel bad, such as, "It made me think that you don't respect me." But you don't have to add the reason. You don't want to be told that you are too sensitive, or that such behaviors shouldn't bother you. All you want to know is whether the person will stop hurtful behaviors.

On the other hand, destructive criticism is global in its focus. It attacks the person and uses words like "always" and "never" to put the other person down. "You" language, such as "you should . . ." is the language of destructive criticism. "You should . . ." makes your words personal and much like a lecture. None of us like someone to lecture us, or to be put down.

Practice your constructive criticism and watch your communication skills improve.

Levels of Communication

In his book, *Why Am I Afraid to Tell You Who I Am?*, John Powell talks about levels of communication that are barriers that keep each of us from understanding the other.

First Level — This level includes clichés, such as "Hi, how're you doing?" and "How are you?" This form of communication shows the other person that you are friendly and that you will do the person no harm or, more appropriately, that you are not a threat. The degree of self-disclosure at this level is zero. We reveal next to nothing by making such general, emotionless statements.

Second Level — This level has to do with facts, statements that can be proven. The fact that I am a counselor, or the fact that I am a man, or that bananas grow in bunches called hands can all be proven by some fact — a birth certificate, a newspaper, a diploma, an encyclopedia, or by simple observation, such as someone's height or weight or any other piece of information that can be proven by the laws of evidence. No matter how interesting or enlightening these facts might be, the level of self-disclosure also is minimal to zero.

Third Level — At this level, some self-disclosure takes place. You express opinions that cannot be proven. For instance, I can tell you that Wednesday is my favorite day of the week. Neither of us can prove it; it is just my opinion. Family arguments frequently revolve around this type of communication. One person has an opinion that differs from another's opinion, and both parties argue as if their opinions were facts. A good example of this level of communication was depicted in the TV show *All in the Family*. Archie Bunker would argue with Michael, his "meat head" son-in-law, over differences of opinion. Archie's bigoted opinions and Michael's liberal ones clashed in episode after episode. Neither could prove that one opinion was more valid than the other, so they continued to argue. The communication was based upon "you" statements. "You are a dumb Pollock!" "You are an ignorant racist!" "You should get a job and support my daughter instead of going to school." "You should treat Ma with more respect! She works her tail off for you."

Fourth Level — This is the level of feelings. This is where the "I" language comes in. If I told you that I like the spring because that is when I recovered from my alcoholism, I feel a sense of gratitude ("I" statement) every time I think of my recovery, you know more about me. The level of self-disclosure is high. This is the level of sharing that involves your recovery from alcoholism. This is the kind of sharing that you would do with your sponsor or a friend you can trust. This is the level where healing occurs. Without honest self-disclosure in these safe situations, there will be no recovery. When this level of communication is effective, you can deal with anything.

Fifth Level — This level, the last of the levels, deals with intimate feelings, feelings that are private and individual and probably hidden away in the back of your mind. There may be deep feelings that rise, for instance, when you are doing your fifth step. (This is the step in which you admit to your God, someone else, and to yourself that you have wronged someone and what the wrong was.) Or the feelings that might rise from a talk with your sponsor or a loved one.

I share with you what I experienced early in my recovery. It was springtime. I was walking down the street when I realized that I hadn't had a panic attack in at least a week (remember, I was plagued with them for almost seven years), and I knew, not believed, that I was going to get well. I had a spiritual experience that day. I felt closer to every living thing. I distinctly remember the green leaves on a tree near where I was walking. I had this overwhelming feeling that I was part of every living being, every tree, every bird, everything.

You will have these feelings one day, or something like them, and when you do, you will reach the fifth level in your communication. This sharing of intimate feelings will signal your healing. Accepting your need to do this may save your life. The feelings will be so strong that you will be compelled to share them. You will call your sponsor or buddy or a trusted friend. You will use "I" language and share how you feel about what is happening to you. The healing will become real.

12
Balance is the Key to Sobriety

Sigmund Freud, the father of modern psychiatry, when asked about the secret to happiness, gave the formula three parts: work, love, and play. I realized some years ago that this also is a formula for relapse-prevention. In all the years I have been in and around 12-step programs, the people who relapse are those who are unbalanced in one of these areas. I might add that those who remained sober had at least two of the three areas in focus; play was usually the short leg. Those who were really sober had balanced work, love, and play.

In Chapter Five, we talked about the four instincts — sex, security, prestige, and social contact — and their importance in our lives. They are a natural part of each of us, and, though each of us responds to them in different degrees of attention and passion, we are compelled to respond to those instincts. Here is a plan to make sure your instincts are satisfied so that you are balanced mentally, spiritually, and physically.

Work: The First Leg of the Stool

Think of your recovery as a three-legged stool. One leg is work, one is love, and one is play.

Almost all of the alcoholics with whom I have worked are in some kind of trouble with work when they come into recovery. They have been fired for drinking. They are in danger of losing their jobs because of their drinking. They believe they must drink to cope with their jobs. Work is a key element in our lives. It's been said that work is the only activity that we do eight hours a day. We don't eat eight hours a day. We are not with our families eight hours a day. We don't make love eight hours a day. The only thing we routinely do for at least eight hours a day is our full-time job. Not even sleep can be counted on as an eight-hour occurrence.

Three things can happen to people who work a program of recovery as it relates to work: 1) They handle their present job more capably, and they stay with what they are doing; 2) they choose a new job; or 3) they move in some other vocational direction and begin new training or work toward a degree. I cannot tell you how to manage this leg. Only you can do that. I do, however, encourage you to remember that a healthy work life is critical to the balance of your sobriety stool.

Get a Job

If you have not worked for a while, don't be too concerned about finding the "perfect" job for you. The objective is to start working. All work has dignity. Every job, no matter how menial, requires effort, thought, and concentration. And whether you believe it, the job might be the one best-suited to you at the given time in your life. One of my first jobs in early recovery was working in the mail room of a large insurance company. It wasn't much, but it was what I needed at that particular time. Although the job could have been done easily by any high-school graduate, I had a lot of trouble with it. I had learned to work while I was on drugs. Off the drugs, it took a long time to master the same activity. Even if one drinks only at night, one still feels the effects of the alcohol the next day. Eye/hand coordination, emotional health, and the ability to handle stress are most seriously affected.

Ask yourself these questions in a quiet moment to clarify your difficulties at work. Write your answers.

1.   Are you satisfied with your present job? Why?

2.   Are you underemployed, or is the job too big for you? In what way?

3.   Are you under too much stress? In what way?

4.   Do you need more education and training for this job? What kind of training do you think you need?

5.   Do you want more education and training to better your employment? In what area would you like this training?

Be sure to give complete answers, because thinking through the questions completely and writing full answers will help you to see what you need to do.

What should you do if you don't have a job? If you are in early sobriety, and you haven't worked for a while, then my advice is to find any job that doesn't bother you too much and get into the habit of working. When you are into sobriety for a year or so, then you can start looking for a job that suits you better. As you move into sobriety, your views toward yourself, toward other people and toward society in general will change. It also takes a year or two of concentrated focus on recovery to really get your feet firmly planted on a foundation of reality. You must deal with your recovery and keep it foremost in your mind. You have two jobs on which to focus: your recovery and your employment. As you gain ground in the first, you will become increasingly ready to try new responsibilities and areas in the second. And as you keep focused on the first and get into the habit of working, you are less likely to experience a relapse.

What do you do if you have a job and you want to change careers? If you already are in a career position — you work in a bank, you are a computer programmer, you are a plumber, for instance — and you want to change your trade or profession, my advice remains the same. Wait until you are at least a year into sobriety, then consider if a change is necessary and how to go about it. Before you make any such move, it is wise to discuss it with your sponsor or with some friend you trust.

As you gain control over this important area, you will discover that the control has a ripple effect on other areas of your life, whether you directly work on them or you don't.

Love: The Second Leg of the Stool

Freud thought so much of love that he put love right up there in importance with work and play. For our purposes here, I have broken love into two parts: *Eros* and *agape.**

- *Eros,* which is where "erotic" is born, is sexual, romantic love.

- *Agape,* from the Greek word for "love," is spiritual love, nonsexual love, love from God to us, the type of love referred to in a 12-step program.

What I experienced in early recovery was *agape* love, unconditional love, no strings attached. Examples from AA or Narcotics Anonymous include helping an alcoholic to recover, providing sponsorship, an ongoing commitment. Knowing *agape* love from a sponsor or a group of people in recovery can help to hold your life together when you are out of balance at work or with your family of origin. This kind of love, coupled with a solid 12-step program and consistent, earnest work on the steps, will help your life to become more manageable.

Eros love, the romantic love, is probably the single most disruptive factor for recovering alcoholics. Once again, I recommend that you avoid such emotional attachments for at least the first year of your sobriety, because in the critical first year, the recovering alcoholic — you — is more likely to replace one addiction (alcohol) with another (a romantic liaison). In this case, I am talking about starting a new relationship. If you are married, or are in a relationship before entering a 12-step program, your case would be different. You would need to check with your sponsor for the particulars on this.

---

*Instead of *philos,* which is brotherly love, I have chosen *agape* to describe this spiritual type of love because originally it meant God's love of man and because the 12-step journey is a spiritual one.

The romantic kind of love is essential, but in early recovery, it is far more important to your balance and to your sobriety to know the love of a friend or a buddy. Unfortunately, the first thing that people who experience a relapse do is to isolate themselves from the people they need the most. Some never developed friends or found a buddy in the first place. It is my firm belief that if you have healthy friends with whom you spend time, share and go to meetings, you will recover.

Meetings Are Not the Cure All

On the other end of the spectrum are the people who are sober for about a year and either do not date, or they stay in destructive relationships because they are afraid to change. They think that if they just go to the meetings, then everything will be all right. Well, it won't be all right. Trust my experience on this point. Meetings alone will not help you or anyone. Eventually, each of us has to deal with this issue of *Eros* love, because the *agape* love of meetings and sponsors and buddies won't meet the need forever. Eventually, you must accept the risk of meeting someone, making the overtures, handling the give and take of such a relationship, and entering into the intimacy of a sexual relationship. *Eros* love is an instinct that must be satisfied. Also, if you are in a bad marriage, this is the time to work on it. Go for counseling. Do whatever it takes, but don't stay stuck in a bad situation.

Ask yourself these questions when evaluating your relationship:

1. Do I need a relationship at this time? Why, or why not?

2.   Does this relationship need improvement? In what way?

3.   Now that I know more about myself, what kind of relationship would I like to have?

Write your answers, because writing the answers will help you to focus on your needs — intellect over emotion.

Attend to this part of your life when the time comes, but give yourself at least a year of sobriety before you make any major change in any significant relationship.

Play: The Third Leg of the Stool

All too frequently, people do not consider play to be important, which is probably why play often is left out of Freud's recipe for happiness. Don't allow yourself to slip into this pattern. Relapse can occur just as quickly when play is eliminated as it can if either of the other legs is out of balance. All three legs must be equal if your stool of sobriety is to remain stable. Play allows us to recreate our energy, our perspective, our interest in life.

The challenge for us alcoholics is that we don't know how to play. Why is that? Because the only play we know is our addiction, getting high with our substance(s) of choice. In recovery, alcoholics may become workaholics, and they wrongly believe that work can be the same as play. Work as play does not have the same effect on your recovery and staying healthy as does play (recreation). You and I both need down time, time when we can be ourselves, relax and have fun. Participating in a competitive sport can be play. Learning something new can be play. Music and reading can be play. Going to a concert can be play. Play is a kind of rest for your brain, your body, and your spirit.

When I had sobered up, I looked around for things that would stimulate my interest. As a kid, I would lift weights, but I didn't accomplish much. When I was sober a few years, I decided to give weight lifting a try again. In the beginning, I was so intimidated because of all the muscular guys in the gym that it took me a whole year to go down to the free-weight room, where they kept the barbells and dumbbells. I would stay upstairs with the weight machines. I regained my courage and overcame my old nemesis "fear" by using the steps outlined in Chapter 10. Gradually, I worked up nerve and joined all the big guys. Ten years later, I continue to work out, I have added about 10 pounds of muscle, and I stay in balance. It is my hobby.

Hobbies, leisure activities, play all have one thing in common: You do them for the sheer pleasure of it and to keep your sobriety stool in balance.

The conclusion of our journey is close at hand. Turn the page, and I'll meet you there.

Conclusion

We started our journey together by defining the problem, the disease. We said that the disease has two parts: the compulsion and the obsession. The compulsion has to do with the physical allergy to the substance that feeds our addiction. First you take a drink, then the drink takes a drink, and, finally, the drink takes you. The obsession is your mind telling you that you must have the drink, and all you can think about is taking a drink. The disease of alcoholism is part of you through your genes or through a variety of other factors. Although you did not "catch" alcoholism, as you might catch a cold or the measles, you are responsible for treating the disease and making yourself healthy.

We briefly considered:

1. The three stages of alcoholism — the adaptive, the dependent, and the deteriorative — which can lead to your death if they continue, unabated by some method of intervention.

2. The Law of Identity in which A=A. A thing is a thing and not something else. The addiction to alcohol (drugs, food, relationships, etc.) and the addict are just that, they are not something else, no matter how strongly they declare that they are.

3. The importance of honesty, and that honesty is the key to all personal growth. Honesty gave me the way to deal with reality. It does for many of us; it probably will work for you, too. I learned the truth about myself and my surroundings. With honesty, I have everything; without honesty, I have nothing. The same is true for you.

4.   The basics of recovery: H.A.L.T.; people, places and things; and bring the body, the mind will follow, to touch upon a few.

5.   The 12 steps, which are among the most powerful forms of therapy to come along for us alcoholics. We worked the steps together, at least it is my deepest hope that you worked them with me. If you did not, begin now to reread this book and to get serious about your sobriety.

6.   The importance of sponsors and how to get them, about buddies, and how to work a meeting for maximum exposure, as far as meeting people goes.

7.   How panic attacks can be cured.

8.   The six-step method for identifying and dealing with feelings and how necessary it is for you to deal with your feelings.

9.   The need for assertiveness and the importance of expressing yourself, how to confront someone, how to use "I" language, how to deal with the there-and-then issues that resurface as though they are part of today.

10. The importance of keeping your three-legged stool of sobriety in balance. Work, love, and play must each have a part in your life for you to achieve good health over your disease.

As I said when we began this journey, these techniques have been derived from my experiences. I am not offering vague theory or the final word in alcoholism treatment. I offer you things that work. I know from experience that if you focus on these techniques and work at them consistently and diligently, you will achieve sobriety and a new life. It can be quite a remarkable life if you want it to be — free from fear and self-doubt and a life in which you can find true meaning and purpose.

To illustrate my point, I'll share one more story. Pretend for a moment that you are lost in the wilderness, and the only piece of navigation equipment you have is a sextant, a device that depends upon sighting the North Star. You take a reading and conclude that if you stay on your northerly course, you will, more than likely, come to civilization. Your civilization is sobriety. If you stay on course toward your goals and your dreams, using the 12-steps, stress management, assertiveness, feelings, and the other techniques reviewed in this book, you will achieve sobriety. Careful practice on the techniques will keep you moving your life from unmanageability to manageability.

There will be times when you are discouraged, when you will want to give up, times when you think that all of this focus on steps and meetings and assertiveness and all the other techniques are just not worth it. Such times come to all of us who are trying to achieve and to maintain sobriety. This might sound a little hokey, but when these times come and you literally fall to your knees in discouragement and despair, think of me. Listen deep inside you and hear, beyond the beat of your heart, my voice telling you to "Get up! Get up! You can do it! Give it one more try!" I have been there. I know the pain. I know the hard work. I know what it takes to find the miracle. Don't give up before you achieve yours. Claim this power in yourself, the last place most people look for it. The power is waiting there for you.

Appendix A
Bibliography

Big Book of Alcoholics Anonymous, 3rd ed. New York: Alcoholics Anonymous World Services Inc., 1976.

Dr. Bob and the Good Oldtimers: A Biography with Recollections of Early A.A. in the Midwest. New York: Alcoholics Anonymous World Services Inc., 1980.

Fritz, Robert. *The Path of Least Resistance.* (Audiotape). Chicago: Nightingale-Conant Corporation.

Gold, Mark S. *The Facts About Drugs and Alcohol.* New York: Bantam Books, 1988.

Jellinek, E. M. *The Disease Concept of Alcoholism.* New Haven, Conn.: Hillhouse Press, 1960.

Lair, Jess. *I Ain't Much, Baby, But I'm All I've Got.* New York: Fawcett Crest, 1975.

Martin, Joseph C. *Chalk Talks on Alcohol.* San Francisco: Harper San Francisco, a division of Harper Collins Publishers, 1989.

Milam, James R. and Katherine Katcham. *Under the Influence: A Guide to Myths and Realities of Alcoholism.* New York: Bantam Books, 1988.

Packer, Edith. *The Art of Introspection.* (Audiotape). Milford, Conn.: Second Renaissance Books.

Peck, M. Scott. *The Road Less Traveled: A New Psychology of Love, Traditional Values and Spiritual Growth.* New York: Simon & Schuster, 1978.

Peele, Stanton. *The Diseasing of America: Addiction Treatment Out of Control.* Boston: Houghton Mifflin Company, 1989.

Rogers, Ronald and Scott C. McMillan. *Don't Help: A Positive Guide to Working with the Alcoholic.* New York: Bantam Books, 1988.

Ross, Elizabeth Kubler. *On Death and Dying.* New York: Simon and Shuster, 1991.

Szasz, Thomas. *The Myth of Mental Illness.* New York: Harper Collins, 1984.

Smith, Manuel. *When I Say No I Feel Guilty.* New York: Bantam Books, 1985.

Tracy, Brian. *The Psychology of Achievement.* (Audiotape). Chicago: Nightingale Conant Company, 1985.

Treego, Ben, and Charles H. Kepner. *The Rational Manager: A Systematic Approach to Problem Solving and Decision Making.* New York: McGraw-Hill Books, 1965.

Wilson, Bill. *Twelve Steps and Twelve Traditions: An Interpretive Commentary on the A.A. Program.* New York: Alcoholics Anonymous World Services, 1976.

Weeks, Claire. *Hope and Help for Your Nerves.* New York: Penguin Books USA.

Appendix B
Suggested Readings

Alcohlics Anonymous. New York: World Services, 1976. This is really the only book that I would make mandatory reading. Do not do what I did and so many people do, which is to not really study it. How to do the steps is described in the *Big Book*, as it is called.

Twelve Steps and Twelve Traditions. New York: World Services. An interpretive commentary on the A.A. program by a co-founder of Alcoholics Anonymous, World Services, Inc. These, as Charlie and Joe point out, are primarily essays on the steps. Very good spiritual information. It is basically a composite of all the major religions and philosophies of the world combined. Do not read it on your own; just go to one step meeting a week, as I have said, and let the "steps work you." Also, do not skip the traditions. There is good stuff there too.

Came to Believe. New York: World Services. This book is a compilation of experiences of 75 A.A.s describing their spiritual awakening and how they found a God of their own understanding. A very valuable addition to the *Big Book* and *Twelve and Twelve.* Ask around and try to find a

"Came to Believe" meeting. It will make a valuable addition to your program.

Brown, Tom Jr. *The Way of the Scout.* New York: Berkley, 1995. Any of his books as well as his field-guide series. When Tom Brown was eight years old, he met his friend's grandfather, an Apache Indian named Stalking Wolf, who taught him how to track. Read about the spirit that moves through all things. It will help your 12-step program a lot.

Charlie and Joe. *The Big Book Discussion.* These tapes made the *Big Book* come alive for me. They will for you too. Check recovery magazines or ask people at the meetings where to order them.

Glasser, William. *Reality Therapy.* New York: Harper & Row, 1965. The premier book to read about responsibility and excuses. Simple, to the point, direct; goes right to the core of what works and what does not.

Gold, Mark. *The Facts About Alcohol and Drugs,* 3rd ed. New York: Bantam Books, 1989. Good, simple advice on alcohol and drugs. Good also for understanding the drug model that we talked about.

Guys, Benjamin Hoff. *The Tao of Pooh.* New York: Penguin Books. Do not do what I did and be turned off by the children's cartoon character Pooh Bear. This book will explain Taoism to you like none I have ever read. An excellent book. It will also help your program a lot.

Lair, Jess. *I Ain't Well, But I Sure Am Better.* New York: Facett. I believe the book is still in print. Read what he has to say about mutual need therapy and why it is so important to have friends. Jess says five friends is the best number to have. Also read the other books by Jess Lair including *I Ain't Much, Baby, But I'm All I've Got.*

Leonard, George. *Mastery: The Keys to Success and Long-Term Fulfillment.* New York: Dutton, 1991. When George Leonard was 48 years old, he took up Aikido and it transformed his life. Read what the author has learned about mastery from his study of Aikido.

Milam, James R. and Katherine Ketcham. *Under the Influence: A Guide to the Myths and Realities of Alcoholism.* New York: Bantam Book published by arrangement with Madrona Publishers, 1983. The best book on the disease concept I have ever read. Read this book and you will know more about the disease concept of alcoholism than 90 percent of the people you will run into. Although I don't agree with everything the author says, it is still a very good book.

Mungus, Gerald. *How To Get Out Of Debt And Live Prosperously.* New York: Bantam/Doubleday Dell, 1990. Basic advice on how to get out of debt using many of the concepts that we talked about: H.A.L.T., inventory, the First Step, etc. I should have read this book sooner. It has helped me a lot. I highly recommend it.

Norris, Chuck. *The Secret Power Within: Zen Solutions to Real Problems.* Boston: Little, Brown, and Co., 1996. Believe it or not, this book is dynamite. I have read a few books on Zen, but never really understood it until I read Chuck's book. Very inspirational reading from the premier martial arts star. Zen has a lot of similarities to the program. A must-read. Also good for the martial arts examples.

Packer, Edith. Audiotapes. A devotée of the teachings of Ayn Rand. She has said some excellent things about therapy and although I do not agree with everything she says, I agree with much of it. This is where I gathered the information about feelings. Books and tapes can be purchased from The Jefferson School, P.O. Box 2934, Laguna Hills, CA 92654.

Rand, Ayn. *The Virtues of Selfishness*. New York: Signet/New American Library, 1964. *The Romantic Manifesto,* 2nd ed. New York: Signet, 1975. Any of her writings, particularly her non-fiction works are very helpful. Some people have asked me how can I read Ayn Rand and although I do not endorse everything she says (for instance, she was a staunch atheist), in a time when it was very, very controversial to talk about selfishness, Ayn Rand was the first to do it. Also, reading any of her works is like taking a course in how to think. Good grounding in the "I/E" concept that we talked about. If it is too confusing for you, drop it until you get a few years of sobriety.

Rogers, Ronald, and Claudia Scott McMillan. *Don't Help: A Positive Guide to Working with the Alcoholic.* New York: Bantam Books, 1988. A positive guide to working with alcoholics; a good no-nonsense approach to counseling. Incorporates all of the things I have talked about. Note particularly the section on identify, don't compare. Very good stuff.

Smith, Manuel. *When I Say No, I Feel Guilty*. New York: Bantam Books, 1985. Learn the basics of assertiveness training from the book that started the assertiveness movement in the '70s. Good no-nonsense advice on how to communicate.

Weeks, Claire. *Hope and Help for Your Nerves, Peace From Nervous Suffering* or *More Hope and Help for Your*

Nerves. New York: Penguin Books. Good solid advice from a truly great woman and scientist. The techniques she teaches are fully compatible with 12-step techniques. Although the writings are a little dated, they are still packed with powerful information. These are the books that have saved my life; they can do the same for you.

About the Author

Barry Bocchieri, M.A., CAC has over 16 years experience as a master's level certified alcoholism counselor. He began his own personal recovery over 16 years ago. Everything he writes about in this book he has lived.

An expert in the field of substance abuse and addiction, he conducts seminars and workshops that are universally well received by all who attend. It has been said he has the unique ability of explaining complex psychological, philosophical, and spiritual concepts in clear, concise, and easy-to-understand language.

Things That Work, has been designed so that it is the only book you have to read for your recovery, with the possible exception of the books *Alcoholics Anonymous* and the *Twelve Steps and Twelve Traditions*. If you like you can supplement *Things That Work* with the other books recommended. Some clients do one and some do the other. The choice is yours. Good luck!

Please send your questions, comments, or feedback to the author at P.O. Box 1136, Edison, NJ 08818-1136.